New Casebooks

WAITING FOR GODOT
and
ENDGAME

New Casebooks

New Casebooks

WAITING FOR GODOT and ENDGAME

SAMUEL BECKETT

EDITED BY STEVEN CONNOR

MACMILLAN

First published 1992 by
THE MACMILLAN PRESS LTD
Houndmills, Basingstoke, Hampshire RG21 2XS
and London
Companies and representatives
throughout the world

ISBN 0–333–54602–4 hardcover
ISBN 0–333–54603–2 paperback

A catalogue record for this book is available
from the British Library.

Printed in Hong Kong

Reprinted 1993

Contents

Acknowledgements

The editor and publishers wish to thank the following for permission to use copyright material:

Mary Bryden, essay 'Gender in transition: *Waiting For Godot* and *Endgame*', by permission of the author;

James L. Calderwood, 'Ways of Waiting in *Waiting for Godot*', *Modern Drama*, 29 (1986), by permission of the University of Toronto;

Steven Connor, 'The Doubling of Presence' in *Samuel Beckett: Repetition, Theory and Text* (1988), by permission of Basil Blackwell Ltd;

Jane Alison Hale, '*Endgame:* How Are Your Eyes?' in *The Broken Window: Beckett's Dramatic Perspective* (1989). Copyright © 1987 by Purdue Research Foundation, by permission of Purdue University Press;

Sylvie Debevec Henning, edited extract from 'Variations on the Hermeneutic Theme' in *Beckett's Critical Complicity: Carnival, Contestation and Tradition* (1988), by permission of the University Press of Kentucky;

Wolfgang Iser, 'Counter-sensical Comedy and Audience Response in Beckett's *Waiting for Godot*', *Gestos*, 4 (1987), by permission of the author;

Andrew K. Kennedy, edited extract from 'Action and Theatricality in *Waiting for Godot*' in *Samuel Beckett* (1989), by permission of Cambridge University Press;

Paul Lawley, 'Adoption in *Endgame*', *Modern Drama*, 31:4 (1988), by permission of the University of Toronto Press;

Jeffrey Nealon, 'Samuel Beckett and the Postmodern: Language Games, Play and *Waiting for Godot*', *Modern Drama*, 31:4 (1988), by permission of the University of Toronto Press;

Judith A. Roof, 'A Blink in the Mirror: From Oedipus to Narcissus and Back in the Drama of Samuel Beckett' in Katherine H. Burkman (ed.), *Myth and Ritual in the Plays of Samuel Beckett* (1987), Farleigh Dickinson University Press, by permission of Associated University Presses;

Gabriele Schwab, edited extract from 'On the Dialectic of Closing and Opening in *Endgame*', *Yale French Studies*, 67 (1984), by permission of Yale French Studies.

Every effort has been made to trace all the copyright holders but if any have been inadvertently overlooked the publishers will be pleased to make the necessary arrangement at the first opportunity.

General Editors' Preface

The purpose of this series of Casebooks is to reveal some of the ways in which contemporary criticism has changed our understanding of commonly studied texts and writers and, indeed, of the nature of criticism itself. Central to the series is a concern with modern critical theory and its effect on current approaches to the study of literature. Each New Casebook editor has been asked to select a sequence of essays which will introduce the reader to the new critical approaches to the text or texts being discussed in the volume and also illuminate the rich interchange between critical theory and critical practice that characterises so much current writing about literature.

The focus of the New Casebooks is on modern critical thinking and practice, with the volumes seeking to reflect both the controversy and the excitement of current criticism. Because much of this criticism is difficult and often employs an unfamiliar critical language, editors have been asked to give the reader as much help as they feel is appropriate, but without simplifying the essays or the issues they raise.

The project of New Casebooks, then, is to bring together in an illuminating way those critics who best illustrate the ways in which contemporary criticism has established new methods of analysing texts and who have reinvigorated the important debate about how we 'read' literature. The hope is, of course, that New Casebooks will not only open up this debate to a wider audience, but will also encourage students to extend their own ideas, and think afresh about their responses to the texts they are studying.

John Peck and Martin Coyle
University of Wales, Cardiff

Introduction

STEVEN CONNOR

Samuel Beckett is among the most written about of all writers and his work continues to attract vast amounts of interpretation, criticism and theory. And yet this is in the face of (and, we must suspect, partly because of) Beckett's reluctance to be drawn into discussion of his own work, indeed his resistance to the very idea of criticism and interpretation as such. In a now-famous letter to the theatre director Alan Schneider in which he politely declined to give any guidance as to the meaning and significance of the characters and setting of his play *Endgame*, Beckett declared, with a kind of scornful fatigue:

> We have no elucidations to offer of mysteries that are all of their ['critics'] own making. My work is a matter of fundamental sounds (no joke intended) made as fully as possible, and I accept responsibility for nothing else. If people want to have headaches among the overtones, let them. And provide their own aspirin.[1]

In fact, earlier in his career, Beckett seems to have seriously contemplated taking up the life of an academic and critic himself, for he held a fellowship for two years at the École Normale Supérieure in Paris and taught for a while at Trinity College, Dublin. In the end, however, his choice was, as he put it in a poem of 1934, for 'years of wandering', over 'the loutishness of learning'.[2] Beckett's amused disdain for the work of criticism and interpretation surfaces through his work as well as outside it, for he makes the climax of the exchange of insults between Vladimir and Estragon the jeer of 'Crritic!!'[3] This mistrust of criticism and interpretation seems to rest on a more generalised mistrust of knowledge and its assumed

1

powers; for a writer who has embraced disorder, uncertainty, and the condition of not knowing, the loutishness of learning must seem to consist precisely in its spurious claims to exercise power and interpretative command over the world. Learning may pretend to the command of a Pozzo, but it is really as helpless to order and understand the perplexities of existence as Lucky is in his broken, rambling disquisition.

And yet, reading and interpretation of Beckett's work go on unabated, just as, in *Waiting for Godot*, Vladimir and Estragon have no choice but to continue asking questions of their world. Indeed, Beckett's work has been the object of a whole range of new theoretical approaches developed over the last two or three decades, which this collection of essays is intended to reflect. In so far as any act of criticism and interpretation and any literary theory rest on the aspiration to completeness of understanding (for who would honestly prefer a theory which explained less to one that explained more?), this only intensifies the deeply ironic division between Beckett's work and the critical reading of it.

But there is a sense in which Beckett's work may be said to have anticipated many more forms of contemporary literary theory and even given them a sort of legitimacy. For what characterises much of the most recent literary theory has been its willingness precisely to' question the forms of authority and command invested in theory itself. Contemporary theory takes for granted – or attempts to, for the thing is more difficult than it sounds – its own relativity. The subject of much contemporary theory is therefore what has been called the 'resistance to theory' and such theory is often as suspicious of the claim to have arrived at final or absolute truth as any Beckett character.[4] Beckett's preference for intellectual 'wandering' over the safe rootedness of theory is perhaps inherited in a metaphorical way by the French philosopher and sociologist Michel Foucault, whose work opened up new avenues of enquiry in history and the social sciences because of its refusal to stay within the established and precomprehended territories of theory. 'After all,' Foucault declares, 'what would be the value of the passion for knowledge, if it resulted in a certain amount of knowledgeableness and not, in one way or another and to the extent possible, in the knower's straying afield of himself?'[5]

If it is the attempt to explore and dramatise the condition of 'straying afield' from oneself, rather than the condition of home-bound certainty that characterises Beckett's work, this never amounts to a simple abandonment of the quest for knowledge and certainty. If all Beckett's characters are ruined philosophers of a kind, they continue to live their ruination philosophically, that is to say, restlessly asking *why* things should be this way. And if Beckett's work enacts, as so many have supposed it does, the collapse of the metaphysical certainties that have sustained Western thought over the last two thousand years and before – the belief in God, in the unity of the world, in the knowability of experience, the communicability of reality through language, the idea of 'man', and the corresponding notion of his historical purpose or destination – then it does so, as it were, from the inside rather than from the outside of these things.

Sylvie Debevec Henning takes something like this view of Beckett's work, suggesting that it contests dominant traditions of thought in a 'dialogic' and 'carnivalesque' way. These terms derive from the work of the influential Soviet critic Mikhail Bakhtin, who argued in a number of works on literature and language written during the 1930s and 1940s that language is always in a condition of struggle, a struggle between multiple voices, styles, idioms and the differential human experiences they embody. This 'dialogic' dimension of language operates against all attempts to unify or centralise language and language use (for example in the idea of a 'correct' or 'standard' English), which normally work by the illegitimate exclusion of linguistic minorities and nonconforming groups. The force of the dialogic is nowhere better illustrated for Bakhtin than in the practices of popular medieval carnival, which, through caricature, craziness and festive carnality, provocatively and sanatively turn the stable rational meanings of the official world upside down.

Sylvie Debevec Henning's argument in *Beckett's Critical Complicity: Carnival, Contestation and Tradition*, from which the essay reprinted later in this volume (essay 7) is taken, is that Beckett's work exists in a 'dialogic' relationship to the abstracting and systematising tendencies of Western philosophical traditions. This is to say that it is best thought of as continuing and contesting those tendencies at the same time, rather than attempting simply to do away with them. This doubleness seems amply borne out by *Waiting for Godot* and *Endgame*. Both are plays which seem to refuse any attempt to impose meaning systematically, and both are visions of irrational and unrationalisable processes – sheer waiting without end or outcome, pure decay without the possibility of death. And yet these experiences of shapelessness and purposelessness are given powerful and distinctive shape by the extraordinarily austere and disciplined dramatic structures in the two plays, with their elaborate repetitions, parallels and patternings of various kinds (when Beckett came to direct *Waiting for Godot* late in his life, his instinct was to emphasise these patternings even more than ever before). Beckett's relationship to theory is perhaps the same as his relationship to rationality more generally; his work attempts to undermine rational comprehension from within rationality, turning logical structures against themselves and using words (since there is no choice but to) to express inexpressibility.

For Sylvie Debevec Henning, as for many of the critics and theorists who have considered Beckett's work in recent years, this mixture of solemnity and playfulness, or catastrophic nihilism and carnival fertility, has striking parallels with the condition of theory itself – indeed, Henning suggests in her introductory chapter that her book attempts to be as much an imitation of Beckett's writing style as an account of it, seeking to follow through that writing in all its comic false starts, digressions and irregularities, without integrating them into any 'single, comprehensive thesis, schema, system, or perspective'.[6] The particular mixture of austerity and playfulness in Beckett's work has attracted other writers eager to expand the possibilities of critical or theoretical writing. Notable among these is Ihab Hassan, who sees in Beckett's work one of the inaugurations of what he and plenty of others call 'postmodernism'.[7] Postermodernism in this sense signifies the rejection of the modernist notion that a work of art should aspire to be absolute, transcendent value, offering a fugitive example of smoothly harmonised unity, coherence and meaning in a world in which such things are no longer to be found. In the joke about the trousers told by Nagg in *Endgame*, Beckett offers a perfect summary of this modernist aesthetic of reparation, in which the artist makes up for the obstinately chaotic nature of the world by the perfection of his artifice; the artist-tailor, confronted by a customer demanding angrily to know why he has taken three months to finish making a pair of trousers when God made the world in six days, replies, scandalised, 'But my dear Sir, my dear Sir, look – at the world – and look – at my TROUSERS'.[8] Beckett had thought enough of this joke to quote its punchline in a critical article that he wrote for the journal *Cahiers d'art* in 1945.[9] But in fact Beckett's work is much more accurately thought of, not as a retreat from chaos and indeterminacy, but as an attempt to enact them. We might perhaps say that the modernist trousers of Nagg's story have been anticipated by the ludicrous incident which concludes *Waiting for*

Godot, where Estragon discusses hanging himself with Vladimir, not realising that his trousers have fallen around his ankles. Here, the crumpled heap of the trousers seem to stand for absolute indignity and foolishness, rather than the aesthetic idealism which they seem to represent in the story of the tailor. The trousers are the sign of man's vanity and mortality; to use the distinction so helpfully proposed by Alan Wilde in his book on modernism and postmodernism, *Horizons of Assent,* the trousers in *Waiting for Godot* seem less a modernist symptom of a world in need of mending, than a postmodernist acknowledgement of a world beyond repair.[10] (Ludicrous and inconsequential though the incident may seem, Beckett took the falling trousers very seriously indeed. Hearing that, at the first performances of *Waiting for Godot* in Paris 1953, Estragon had kept his trousers half on, Beckett wrote a letter to Roger Blin, the director of the play, insisting that 'He mustn't. He absolutely mustn't' and that in future performances the trousers should fall abjectly 'around the ankles'.[11])

Where modernist works, like those, for example, of Beckett's great friend and master, James Joyce, constitute an act of supreme making, postmodernist works like those of Beckett constitute an art of unmaking, a playful 'literature of silence' as Ihab Hassan has put it.[12] Looked at in this way, Estragon's miserable 'Nothing to be done'[13] at the opening of *Waiting for Godot* may signify more than just Estragon's frustration with his boot: it may be a prediction that this play will be an enactment of vacuity, a 'nothing' which has still nevertheless to be gone through, for audience and performers, must still be 'done', in order that it can be, as we say, 'done with'. The words predict accurately the rhythm of this play and others in Beckett's work, which first weave together a pattern and then proceed to unweave it, in a dramatic version of the strange and wonderful machines produced by the French sculptor Jean Tinguely that are designed to consume themselves.

Nevertheless, whatever extreme of the aesthetics of absence or self-annihilation art may aspire to, it is difficult for it to 'do' absolutely 'nothing', and perhaps especially in the theatre, where something will always, ineradicably, have been done. What will have happened may only have been a sort of empty game, 'just play' as a character says in a later work by Beckett which is itself called, just *Play.* But the theory and criticism of postmodernism has been compelled by writers such as Beckett to take game-playing in art and literature more seriously than before. Indeed, the idea of the game has been central in the theory of the postmodern put forward by the French philosopher Jean-François Lyotard, who interestingly suggests that postmodernism involves an abandonment of the idea of absolute truth, since the possibility of attaining to such a truth is crucially dependent on there being a language in which to do so. But there is no such thing as single language, suggests Lyotard. Language – and social life and communication in general – consists rather in the unpredictable slips, shifts and struggles between 'language-games', a term that Lyotard borrows from the early twentieth-century philosopher of language, Ludwig Wittgenstein. The aim of these games is not so much to describe the world truthfully, as to bring about certain effects or aims. One of the most influential of Lyotard's notions, and one that connects interestingly with the ideas of Mikhail Bakhtin, is that we should not seek to do violence to the multiplicity of language-games (dialects, specialised, unorthodox, or private languages, for example) by subordinating them within any one linguistic frame, but should rather encourage the openness of their play.[14] For Jeffrey Nealon, in the essay on *Waiting for Godot* reprinted in this volume (essay 3), the openness to the play of language-games in Beckett's drama constitutes a positive rather than a merely melancholy loss of fundamental certainties. Nealon offers the surprising, but hopeful judgement that Estragon and Vladimir have, in their own words, not so much lost their metaphysical beliefs, as got rid of them. 'Waiting for legitimation of their society in Godot is, from the beginning, unnecessary; they constitute a society which is always already formed by their participation in language games.'[15] Gabriele Schwab focuses in a slightly different way upon the idea of language-games, in her essay on *Endgame* reprinted below (essay 6). Her emphasis is not so much upon the socially cohesive effects of the language-games played by Hamm and Clov as on their fragmentation, multiplicity and unpredictability.[16]

Before he turned to the theatre in the late 1940s, Beckett had been primarily a writer of fiction, and, indeed, continued to write fiction (and poetry) alongside his work for the theatre until his death in 1989. Since the appearance of *Waiting for Godot*, Beckett's fame has rested much more upon his work for the stage than on his work for the page, and this may have something to do with the sheer difficulty of much of Beckett's prose, which ruthlessly denies itself and its reader any of the usual appurtenances of character and narrative; his novel *The Unnamable*, for example, is the monologue of a being who has no clear idea who he is, where he is, or even whether he has a body (and therefore whether or not he is a 'he'). His work having been pushed to this extreme of impalpability, the theatre provided a relief for Beckett (and, we might suggest, for his critics and readers too). In the theatre, he once said, 'one is working with a certain space and with people in this space', where there seems always to be some undeniable presence.[17] A recent generation of Beckett criticism has turned away from philosophical interpretation of Beckett's works, the enquiry into what the plays *mean*, and towards the investigation of the experience of the drama itself, without attempting to transform that experience into something else. This approach is represented in this volume by the work of Andrew Kennedy (essay 1), who attends closely to the experience of the plays in the theatre and especially to what may be called their 'self-conscious theatricality', their refusal to suggest that the 'certain space' of the plays is anywhere else but a stage, and their stress on the purity of theatrical action in itself. For Kennedy, it is the way in which this denuded and unpromising space is filled with human action and meaning – with games, jokes, songs, disputes, reconciliations – which is the most important quality of *Waiting for Godot*. The theatrical space of *Waiting for Godot* is therefore both provisional and definite, to correspond with the two common meanings of the word 'certain'. Despite all of the uncertainties about what happens in it, says Andrew Kennedy, the dramatic experience of the play itself is 'fully embodied'.[18]

Critics influenced by the form of contemporary literary theory known as deconstruction tend to be sceptical of this argument about the immediacy of the plays. Deconstruction, deriving principally from the work of Jacques Derrida, is characterised by its suspicion of 'presence', the idea that anything, a meaning or an experience, can ever be experienced in itself, all at once and immediately. This is an apprehension that is verified by thinking about the experience of the present tense. If there is a sense in which it is true to say that we live only in the present, since the past and the future do not exist, then in another sense this is a profound error. The present tense can never be grasped in itself, because its 'presentness' is always either anticipated in the future, or has already slipped into the past. The purest, and most palpable characteristic of the present is precisely that it is never there, is never pure. Deconstruction is the name of the critical activity that seeks to analyse the paradoxical structure of absence that undermines every attempt to affirm presence, purity, immediacy.

For James Calderwood (essay 2), the experience of *Waiting for*

Godot (which is to say the experience of watching it as well as the experience which it represents) is precisely of this indefiniteness, this feeling of being there and not there at the same time. As opposed to the idea that, in *Waiting for Godot*, the action is complete, pure, and purely itself, Calderwood explicates the paradoxical structure of presence and absence in waiting, that activity in which one is most firmly lodged in the present, and yet also painfully absent from it: 'waiting', he writes, 'which implies the absence of the waited-for, is itself mysteriously absent. Moreover, waiting is a self-erasing non-activity, since it negates the transient activities we engage in while waiting.'[19] James Calderwood's argument is an exemplary exposition of the links between Beckett and the deconstructive theory of Derrida, not least because of the way that, unlike many, it refuses to allow the lazy identification of deconstruction with destruction pure and simple. For Beckett, as for Derrida, nothing is ever *simply* present or *simply* absent.

My own essay on *Waiting for Godot* and *Endgame* (essay 9) attempts to develop a similar kind of argument, though it mounts its critique of the idea of pure theatrical presence by focusing on the idea of repetition rather than the idea of waiting. In Beckett's works, the only way to be sure of anything is to do it again and, if necessary, once more again. But it is in the nature of compulsive repetition to be unsatisfying, since the very need to repeat signals some inadequacy, some imperfection in what is called upon to be repeated. *Waiting for Godot* and *Endgame* not only repeat themselves constantly, in words and actions, but also explore the consolations and disappointments of repetitive behaviour in the characters. Pure presence is impossible in a world in which, on the one hand, nothing can happen once and for all, and, on the other, nothing can be guaranteed as having been accurately repeated.

Gabriele Schwab's discussion of *Endgame* (essay 6) also focuses in a deconstructive manner on Beckett's work, or, we should say, uses Derrida's discussion of openness and closure in language to describe the deconstructive dynamics of that work itself. Derrida suggests that language has two dimensions or characteristics, presence (in which meaning is, or seems, stable and fixed) and difference (for every apparently stable meaning is in fact dependent upon the unstable, because theoretically infinite, forms of difference in a language which establish the possibility of any individual meaning). For Derrida, the possibility of a full, stable and self-present meaning is always threatened by the movement of difference: to put it another way, the closure of final meaning is always threatened by the openness of further interpretation. It is not so much that meaning is simply dissolved or negated by the drift of difference in language (we remember, there is no simple presence or absence in deconstructive theory); it is rather that meaning is only possible because of the structures of difference which both confirm and undermine it. Adopting this perspective, as Gabriele Schwab does, means attending less to *what* a play like *Endgame* might mean (what sort of symbol it is of the human condition) and more to the characteristic rhythms of *how* the play offers meaning and then dissolves it. Seen in this way, the dialectic of closure and openness, the desire to fix upon invariable and all-inclusive interpretations opposed by the way in which those meanings always seem incomplete or unsatisfactory, is not just something that happens to the viewer of *Endgame*, but is also the principal 'action' of the play itself, in which the characters gnaw and nag endlessly at the question of what they mean. Beckett's work proves particularly responsive to this kind of deconstructive analysis precisely because of this self-reflexivity, the fact that the action consists of (failed) acts of interpretation. Vladimir and Estragon, Pozzo and Lucky, Hamm and Clov, Nagg and Nell, are all struggling as hard to read themselves as we are struggling to read them.

Paul Lawley's intriguing account of adoption in *Endgame* (essay 8) is by no means a declared application of deconstructive theory, but it nevertheless evidences a sensitivity to the paradoxical co-presence of contradictions which is typical of deconstructive criticism at its best. Lawley's argument is that the question of genetic legitimacy in the play (who is the son or father of whom) is closely related to the question of narrative legitimacy (whether the stories told in the play are true or invented). In the 'corpsed' world of *Endgame*, the only nature is one that is brought into being and sustained by narrative so that, as Lawley suggests, 'adoption is a figure for the fictional process itself, the only acceptable means of self-perpetuation for characters who reject the processes of nature'. As a consequence, there is a troubling overlap between the stories Hamm tells about family relationship and adoption and those stories themselves, an overlap between the 'narrative of situation' and the 'situation of narrative'. The sharp distinction between the inside and the outside of fictional processes thereby begins to dissolve, in a way that comes to affect our own apprehension of *Endgame* itself, with its own apparently sharp distinction between outer and inner worlds. In a skilful critical manoeuvre, Lawley makes adoption the very centre of a process which 'simultaneously establishes and renders unstable the very ground on which *Endgame* is played out'.[20]

Although deconstructive theory and perhaps contemporary theory in general has focused most closely on questions of reading and interpretation as they are raised by the reading of literary texts, such questions are posed with particular force by the drama, painfully distributed as it always is between the 'closed' condition of the text and the 'open' condition of the performance. Beckett's own attitude to the question of dramatic as opposed to textual interpretation was deeply ambivalent. On the one hand, he could be the most dictatorial of directors (as he is the most fastidious of playwrights when it comes to providing stage directions), demanding an absolute fidelity to the specifications of his text, and, on more than one occasion, disowning productions of his plays that did not meet these requirements. But he could also acknowledge the inevitable openness to chance and uncertainty of the theatrical process – indeed his plays often seem to be dramatisations of these very principles. In fact his last completed work, the play *What Where*, ends with the words 'Make sense who may. I switch off'.[21]

What this brings about is a particularly complex relationship between text and reader or, in the cases of *Waiting for Godot* and *Endgame*, between play and audience. One of the strongest currents in contemporary literary theory in recent decades has been the theory of reader-response or reader-centred meaning, associated particularly with the work of Wolfgang Iser and Stanley Fish. Both of these critics argue strongly, though in different ways, against the idea that texts contain their meanings and significances in and of themselves. For all texts must be read to be understood, which implies that the proper concern of the critic ought not to be with texts themselves, but with the ways in which readers respond to – and thereby construct – texts. In the case of dramatic performance, the situation is more complex, though not fundamentally different in kind, since the performance that the audience responds to and makes sense of is always already a 'reading' of an original text. Indeed, the case of drama is instructive, since it suggests that every reading of a text is like a production or staging of a play, which is to say, neither entirely free nor entirely constrained. No writer has been more concerned with the dynamics of text and reader interaction than Wolfgang Iser, whose essay on *Waiting for Godot* is reprinted here (essay 4). Iser's particular concern is with the dynamics of comic structures, and he offers an analysis of how the audience's troubled laughter at performances of the play relates to the problems of interpretation which the play throws up. Laughter, Iser suggests, is both liberation and mastery; the absurdity and inconsequence of *Waiting for Godot* liberate us momentarily from the demands of consistent rationality and yet also confirm our sense of superiority over the helpless and ridiculous tramps in the play. But our laughter is troubled and uncertain, because we can never be sure that what we are watching is indeed mere nonsense or foolery, and can never attain a consistent interpretative position with regard to the play. Once again, the 'action' of Beckett's play proves to be identical with the action of watching it, or reacting to it; the building up of patterns of coherence which are constantly dissolved.

Jane Alison Hale's 'How Are Your Eyes?' (essay 5) explores another form of undermining common in Beckett's plays, namely its unsettling of the characters' and audience's sense of space, place and position. Hale argues that in this Beckett is playing knowingly with a powerful tradition in Western culture that associates the power and command of reason with the faculty of sight, and especially the fixed distance between the observing subject and the observed world implied by the laws of perspective. By undermining the power of sight to command the world at a distance, Beckett's work is associated with an energetic current of critique in contemporary (especially French) philosophy, which has questioned the 'ocular-centrism' of philosophical accounts of rationality.[22] As Jane Alison Hale's essay makes evident, it is the drama which offers the most conspicuous opportunities for a writer to undermine that link between vision and commanding reason, for the drama is precisely the literary form in which we *see* the action made manifest before us. It is for this reason that a play such as *Endgame* is so powerful and discomfiting; since it stations its audience in this commanding vantage point only to dislodge it.

The commanding gaze, as many have pointed out, is associated not only with reason, but also with the very experience and structure of subjectivity itself. The sense of individual being is closely dependent upon the sense that each of us views the world from a unique point, or 'point of view', even though such a sense is a metaphorical interpretation, or effect of the operations of sight, rather than an accurate physical description of those operations. It is in the work of psychoanalysts such as Sigmund Freud and, more recently, Jacques Lacan in France, that the illusions of the centred and singular self and especially the centring achieved via the operations of sight, have been most notably explored. Judith A. Roof draws on this work in her exploration of the structure of looking in Beckett reprinted in this volume (essay 10). Jacques Lacan called the inaugurating moment of selfhood in infant life the 'mirror-stage', since it takes place when the child sees itself (often in a mirror) for the first time as a unity, rather than as a collection of separate drives and impulses. The mirror stage is both a recognition and a misrecognition for Lacan, since the self can only be known and grasped as a unity through some kind of image, or fiction. Later, the narcissism of this stage gives way to the recognition that the self exists as an object in others' field of vision, and the acknowledgement, after the successful passage through the Oedipus complex, of this fact. In the section from her essay reprinted here, Roof suggests that the many pairs who exist in Beckett's early drama, especially *Waiting for Godot*, *Endgame* and *Happy Days*, enact the relationships of the mirror stage. The important insight offered by Lacan's tragic psychoanalysis, and developed suggestively by Roof in her engagement with Beckett's drama, is that knowledge of possession of self is impossible; the self is constituted out of the very struggle to constitute itself.

Beckett's well-known antipathy to formal politics (he once replied to a questionnaire seeking his political views with the ambiguous words 'Up the Republic') is perhaps one of the reasons why political and especially left-political critics have had little – or little complimentary – to say about his work. Many have felt that Beckett's work, though deeply sensitive to human suffering and exploitation, is too caught up in that suffering and not sufficiently attentive to the particularities of history to be regarded as politically affirmative.[23] There are signs, however, that this attitude is beginning to shift. This has partly to do with a more general shift within theory as a whole, towards that may be called the politics of representation. Where an earlier view of the political landscape had suggested that one could draw a pretty clear distinction between political and historical realities and the cultural forms – language, literature, art in general – which represented those realities, more recent theory has attempted to grasp the material force and importance in themselves of such cultural representations. Central to this is the principle that the ways in which the social and physical world is narrated, pictured and interpreted in very large degree constitute that world. The power of language and representation (who speaks, how, to whom and under what circumstances) is in this sense always political.

Seen in this light, Beckett's undermining of absolute truths and certainties, and his opening up of the abstract and systematising force of rationality to the dissolving forces of the body, and the sheer contingency of existence, cannot help but have profound political significance when such notions of certainty and rationality have regularly been recruited to the side of established power. There are reasons of course why one should beware of seeing the assault on rationality as emancipatory in itself, not least because of the horrifyingly oppressive forms of political irrationalism of which this century provides so many conspicuous examples. Beckett's work may be seen as a dramatisation of what is in the last instance (and perhaps long before that), a problem of power – the problem of how to reconcile the claims of reason with the demands of existence, the rational desire for order and total explanation with the imperative to respect difference and unpredictability.

In no area of cultural politics is this problem of more pressing concern than in feminist theory. This theory typically contests the male identification of masculine experience with essential human experience, along with the denigration or pathologising of female experience which this implies. Contemporary feminist theory is much concerned with the question of whether or not this argument is best conducted by a deconstructive strategy which throws into suspicion the idea of identity as such (including, therefore, the idea that gender exists in itself rather than being constructed through representation). It is because of this deconstructive force, rather than because of its political affirmativeness that Beckett's work is beginning to attract the attention of a number of feminist critics and theorists. Not surprisingly, such theorists have been drawn to his later work for the theatre, such as *Happy Days* (1961), *Not I* (1972), *Footfalls* (1976) and *Rockaby* (1981) which have female protagonists and suggest powerful parallels between Beckett's vision of despair, decentredness and dispossession and female experience as such. Mary Bryden's essay (11), written especially for this collection, takes on the difficult question of the *absence* of the female in *Waiting for Godot* and *Endgame*, arguing that the plays have a feminist force in their assault on the authority of maleness along with the values of rationality and identity compacted with maleness.

The most striking thing about the relationship between Beckett's work and contemporary literary and cultural theory therefore is their mutative reciprocity, their capacity each to anticipate and transform the other. I suspect that, as this theory continues to open up and reread Beckett's work in the manner of the essays represented in this volume, it will keep discovering the ways in which that work itself has helped to create the intellectual and philosophical conditions that have enabled the development of much of contemporary theory. In such a situation, the fixed relationships of work and criticism are thrown into a strange productive turmoil, as we are no longer certain whether we are reading the work or whether it is reading us.

NOTES

1. Samuel Beckett, *Disjecta: Miscellaneous Writings and a Dramatic Fragment*, ed. Ruby Cohn (London, 1983), p. 109.

2. 'Gnome', *Collected Poems in English and French 1930–1978* (London, 1984), p. 7.

3. Samuel Beckett: *Complete Dramatic Works* (London, 1986), p. 69. I have examined the dialogue with criticism that Beckett maintains through his work in 'Beckett and His Critics', *LJ*, 1 (1990), 26–7.

4. Paul de Man has asserted that '[n]othing can overcome the resistance to theory since theory is itself this resistance', *The Resistance to Theory* (Manchester, 1986), p. 19.

5. Michel Foucault, *The Use of Pleasure*, trans. Robert Hurley (Harmondsworth, 1985), p. 8.

6. Sylvia Debevec Henning, *Beckett's Critical Complicity: Carnival, Contestation and Tradition* (Lexington, 1988), p. 7.

7. See Ihab Hassan, 'Joyce-Beckett: A Scenario in 8 Scenes and a Voice', *Paracriticisms: Seven Speculations of the Times* (Urbana, 1975), pp. 63–73.

8. Beckett, *Complete Dramatic Works*, p. 103.

9. 'La Peinture des van Velde ou le Monde et le Pantalon', repr. in *Disjecta*, ed. Ruby Cohn (London, 1983), pp. 118–32.

10. Alan Wilde, *Horizons of Assent: Modernism, Postmodernism, and the Ironic Imagination* (Baltimore and London, 1981), p. 131.

11. Letter quoted in Deirdre Bair, *Samuel Beckett: A Biography* (London, 1980), p. 362.

12. See Ihab Hassan, *The Literature of Silence: Henry Miller and Samuel Beckett* (New York, 1967).

13. Beckett, *Complete Dramatic Works*, p. 10.

14. See Jean-François Lyotard, *The Postmodern Condition: A Report on Knowledge* (1979), trans. Geoffrey Bennington and Brian Massumi

(Manchester, 1984) and *The Differend: Phrases in Dispute*, trans. Georges Van Den Abbeele (Manchester, 1988).

15. See p. 45 below.

16. See pp. 88–9 below.

17. Quoted in *Materialen zu Becketts Endspiel*, ed. Michael Haerdter (Frankfurt, 1968), p. 88. (My translation.)

18. See p. 28 below.

19. See p. 33 below.

20. See p. 126 below.

21. Beckett, *Complete Dramatic Works*, p. 476.

22. See Martin Jay's excellent overview of the ocularcentrism (the term is his) of Western traditions of rationality, and recent critiques of it, in his 'In the Empire of the Gaze: Foucault and the Denigration of Vision in Twentieth-Century French Thought', in *The Foucault Reader*, ed. David Couzens Hoy (Oxford, 1986), pp. 175–204.

23. The notable exception to this is Theodor W. Adorno's essay of 1961, 'Towards an Understanding of *Endgame*', repr. in *Twentieth-Century Interpretations of 'Endgame': A Collection of Critical Essays*, ed. Bell Gale Chevigny (Englewood Cliffs, 1969), pp. 82–114.

1

Action and Theatricality in 'Waiting for Godot'

ANDREW K. KENNEDY

It is not surprising that fourteen hundred convicts of San Quentin penitentiary responded enthusiastically to a performance of Beckett's play (in 1957) – completely strange yet meaningful to them. They could draw on their own experience of waiting, the empty kind of waiting where 'nothing to think about' is a permanent threat, and every happening offers both a promise and a disillusioning repetition of the daily round. They also had fewer preconceptions about what constitutes a well-plotted play than did the literary and theatre-going public of the time.

We are not in the situation of the prisoners of San Quentin; and the risk, in our time and especially for the new reader, is a second-hand or learned response to a 'great modern classic' (an examination set book), over-burdened with often far-fetched commentary. The best starting point for critical discussion is still the immediate experience of the play, guided by searching questions concerning both the text and its context. The stage is almost empty, stripped, as hardly ever since Shakespeare, to present only the bare boards and one tree, which can suggest almost anything from the tree of life to all that is left of 'Nature' in a deserted and desolate landscape. The stage is the stage, it also a road. (It could be a round stage suggesting the circus, but the stage directions do not ask for that.) The opening sequence defines the situation of Vladimir and Estragon clearly enough for a play that is to use 'uncertainty' as an element of composition. Both characters are ageing and weary; they appear to be inseparably linked as a pair, in the symbiotic love–hate relationship of a couple; they are usually dressed as bowler-hatted literary tramps, though the stage directions do not state this; they are also like performing comedians, the straight man and his stooge in cross-talk. Their strong physical presence is underlined by talk of physical discomfort and pain – Estragon's boot problem, Vladimir's urination problem. Metaphysical uncertainty is suggested by their speculative talk about time, place and the purpose of their waiting, about what *is* happening, what might have happened (should they have jumped from the top of the Eiffel Tower some fifty years ago?) and what might happen. Their speech is a mixture of the formal ('Nothing to be done') and the colloquial; the minimally simple and the rhetorical, with a sprinkling of Irishisms ('Get up till I embrace you') and literary or biblical allusion ('Hope deferred maketh the something sick, who said that?'). The collision of levels and styles is controlled, good-humoured and darkly humorous (tragicomic) from the opening scene on.

ACTION IN NON-ACTION

The act of waiting makes us aware of an indirect and ambivalent kind of action that promises an end of the sense of purpose as well as conclusion. Waiting, both in life and in drama, can involve a whole range of experience, from a sense of paralysis to fruitful silence, the empty or the anxious mind trying to cope by inventing distractions. The suspense of melodrama and farce, the long postponements of comedy and the prolonged quest of tragedy (the procrastinations of Hamlet for example) all constitute patterns of waiting.

In Beckett's play, the pattern of waiting is an ingenious combination of expectations and let-downs, of uncertainty and of gradual run-down without end. The expectations of Estragon and Vladimir seem to be both limitless and irrational; and the various climaxes and psuedo-climaxes, or non-arrivals, do not change their condition. But the protagonists, and the audience, are being 'kept going' by playful variations in the pattern of waiting, with uncertainties of meaning and destination. For example, early on we hear Vladimir's speculations on the traditional hope of being saved:

> **Vladimir**   It'll pass the time. (*Pause.*) It was two thieves crucified at the same time as our Saviour. One –
> **Estragon**   Our what?

> **Vladimir** Our Saviour. Two thieves. One is supposed to have been
> saved and the other . . . *(he searches for the contrary of being saved)*
> . . . damned.
> **Estragon** Saved from what?
> **Vladimir** Hell.[1]

['Hell' is later vehemently exchanged for 'death' by Vladimir.]

The whole sequence sounds tentative and open-ended, both in performance and when examined critically. Only one out of three evangelists tells of one thief being saved, and if the silence of the others is a kind of truth, then both thieves may have been damned. The reader/spectator feels that the uncertainty concerning one of the thieves is transferred to the speakers, but without the firm equation we find in *The Pilgrim's Progress* type allegory. It is a haunting and universal image, like a medieval triptych of the Crucifixion with the central panel, the Christ picture, missing. But a direct Christian symbolic interpretation would not be warranted. The allusion to some remote possibility of 'being saved' is not excluded by the text; it reverberates as a concern, an anxious questioning – without nihilistic parody.

The presence of the tree offers no consolation; assumed to be a dead willow by Vladimir, it cannot, at this point, serve even as a landmark. On the contrary, it prompts the first symptoms of fear: being at the wrong place at the wrong time, waiting in vain (pp. 14– 15). The black humour of trying to identify a meeting-place where landmarks get blurred, or trying to distinguish between today and yesterday when all the days of the week merge in 'sameness', defines the first movement of the play. Estragon's *if*'s ('And if he doesn't come?', 'If he came yesterday and we weren't here you may be sure he won't come again today') and his *until* ('until he comes') present the anxieties within this act of waiting at an early stage. The risk of waiting in vain is also emphasised early in the play by the failure of an attempt to clarify the inexorable conditions supposedly set by the supposed Mr Godot. In the course of a long dialogue 'canter' concerning Godot (pp. 18–19), Vladimir is forced to admit, with scathing irony, that they no longer have any 'rights' – 'We got rid of them' ('waived them' in the first edition, French *bazardés*). Meanwhile, every noise brings fear: the wind in the reeds or a shout may usher in the coming of Godot.

So the terrible cry that precedes the arrival of Pozzo and Lucky creates the illusion of Godot's arrival, not just for the protagonists, but for a first audience as well. It turns out to be a supreme diversion, in the double scene of amusing distraction and enforced detour. Throughout this long and centrally placed play-within-the-play the direct act of waiting is suspended: attention shifts to the doings of Pozzo and Lucky, the lord of the waste, and his shrivelled carrier, dancer, thinker, speaker. The abandoned road suddenly takes on the appearance of the old highway of picaresque fiction (as in *Tom Jones*, say): *anything* might happen here, monster-like creatures can traverse this road and enact a cruel spectator sport, watched by Estragon and Vladimir. The compulsions of the long process of waiting are almost forgotten despite Pozzo's occasional speculations about the identity and demands of this personage: 'Godet . . . Godot . . . Godin' (pp. 29, 36). The name of Godot is hushed up with ironic apologies for having taken Pozzo for 'him': ('Personally, I wouldn't even know him if I saw him.' / 'That's to say . . . you understand . . . the dusk . . . the strain . . . waiting . . . I confess . . . I imagined . . . for a second . . .'). At this stage the deepening uncertainty about Godot's appearance and whereabouts tells the audience, significantly, that anyone who comes might be taken for the one who is expected. Thus the act of waiting, which keeps suggesting a quest, has been undertaken on the flimsiest supposition, a casual invitation from an absent host.

The terrible interlude of Pozzo and Lucky 'passes the time' but changes nothing. Soon, the first appearance of the Boy (before the end of Act I) re-enacts and sums up the uncertainties of waiting. In a quiet ritual the Boy appears, like a Messenger in Greek drama, but without any message. For a tense moment, it sounds as if some oracle might be disclosed: 'You have a message from Mr Godot?' / 'Yes, sir.' But the little scene that begins by miming the gesture of a revelation, shifts into an inconclusive cross-examination:

> *Silence.*
> **Vladimir**   You work for Mr Godot?
> **Boy**   Yes, sir.
> **Vladimir**   What do you do?
> **Boy**   I mind the goats, sir.
> **Vladimir**   Is he good to you?
> **Boy**   Yes, sir.
> **Vladimir**   He doesn't beat you?
> **Boy**   No, sir, not me.
> **Vladimir**   Whom does he beat?
> **Boy**   He beats my brother, sir.

Vladimir Ah, you have a brother?
Boy Yes, sir.
Vladimir What does he do?
Boy He minds the sheep, sir.
Vladimir And why doesn't he beat you?
Boy I don't know, sir.
Vladimir He must be fond of you.
Boy I don't know, sir.
Silence.

(p. 51)

The light fusion of myth and realism (trying to track down an elusive person or possibility) sounds 'possible', soothing, almost affirmative. Since no message *has* come down to them, Vladimir will send a message to Mr Godot: 'Tell him ... tell him you saw us. (*Pause.*) You did see us, didn't you?' For the moment, the inconclusive ritual has at least confirmed the existence of Estragon and Vladimir. In that sense the waiting has not been in vain, so far. In the controlled uncertainty of the concluding dialogue of the first act, the Christ image returns ('**Estragon** All my life I have compared myself to him'), along with Estragon's naming of the suicide rope, and vague memories of an earlier existence, some time (fifty years ago perhaps), some place (by the Rhône?). Estragon's serio-comic longing for separation ('We weren't made for the same road') gives way to the curtain image (*They do not move*): separation is both wanted and feared; movement is desired but paralysed; the end is far from ending.

The second act, with its cycle of repetitions and variations, dramatises the ultimate problem of waiting: 'passing the time' without total lethargy. Recharging the batteries of patience is as hard for Estragon and Vladimir as keeping non-action 'going' is for the dramatist.

First, the sense of an 'eternal return' is dramatised by Vladimir's opening round-song ('And dug the dog a tomb') which might as well go on for ever. Then the recognition of Estragon by Vladimir, repeating variants of some phrases from the opening of Act I ('Come here till I embrace you'), also suggests a ritual without end. By contrast, the sudden flowering of the tree, and later Pozzo's blindness and Lucky's dumbness, are *new* events which underline the relentless onward march of time. Yet the movement of time is stilled, or slowed down to the point of stasis, by the sense of a perpetual present, by the circularity of the action, and by the self-conscious efforts of the protagonists to bury time. We watch Estragon and Vladimir jointly trying to tinker with the wheels of time, so to speak. But their perceptions of time are comically opposed (pp. 59–62). For Vladimir, today is firmly 'today', a new day, after the passage of a night spent in solitude but with a degree of happiness. (Perhaps 'happiness' is inseparable from greeting the day as new and distinct, as Winnie is to do in *Happy Days*.) By contrast, Estragon denies the separateness of today and yesterday, and claims a kind of total amnesia; the supposed passage of one night has wiped out his memory of the tree, the attempted suicide, and the arrival of Pozzo and Lucky. All that remains is a blur and a pain. The place itself is not recognised by Estragon; when challenged, he furiously rejects the 'scenery' as a 'muckheap'. The depressed sense of sameness – loss of feeling *for* time and place – has turned the Macon country into the Cackon country, a place of dirt, panic, or general sickness.

The act of waiting makes urgent demands even when those who wait are beginning to lose their feeling of urgency. Their situation may not be hopeless, may even be euphoric – for a moment. Early in the second act, Vladimir invites Estragon (still smarting from being beaten at night, and other grievances) to a little ceremony affirming mutual happiness:

> Vladimir Say, I am happy.
> Estragon I am happy,
> Vladimir So am I.
> Estragon So am I.
> Vladimir We are happy.
> Estragon We are happy. (*Silence.*) What do we do now, now that we are happy?
> Vladimir Wait for Godot. (*Estragon groans. Silence.*) Things have changed since yesterday.
> Estragon And if he doesn't come?
> Vladimir (*After a moment of bewilderment.*) We'll see when the time comes. (*Pause.*)
>
> (p. 60)

Being 'happy', this ironic ritual shows, is not a compulsive need like 'waiting', which has some of the qualities of a total commitment. The prospect of being disappointed time after time – after some fifty years – is shrugged off with that cliché of the optimistic clown: 'We'll see when the time comes.'

The act of waiting becomes both more playful and more desperate in Act II. Self-congratulations for 'success' alternate with cries of anguished lamentation. In a fine succession of verbal games (pp. 62–77) Estragon and Vladimir try out improvised poetry (the line-by-line lyrical repartee on 'the dead voices' / 'like leaves' / 'like sands'); they try contradicting each other, asking further questions, recapitulating the already fading lore of 'yesterday', testing memory, testing the sun and the moon, the cosmos, and, nearer home, the continuity of experience: Estragon's leg-wound and the reality of his boots (the black pair has been replaced by a brown one, as if a practical joker had come in the night). Further games of self-distraction follow: eating a radish (there are no more carrots), trying on the boots, trying to sleep, the hat-game with Lucky's 'thinking' hat, and finally improvising their own acts ('I'll do Lucky, you do Pozzo'), a cursing match, a ritual of reconciliation, and exercises ('doing the tree'). It is this kind of inventiveness that earns Estragon's self-approval:

> We don't manage too badly, eh Didi, between the two of us? [. . .] We always find something, eh Didi, to give us the impression we exist?
> (p. 69)

The 'merry' games of self-distraction are cut across by an intermittent cry. At its simplest, we hear Estragon's repeated 'Ah' as an increasingly desperate response to the 'we are waiting for Godot' refrain. While Estragon is troubled by his nightmare, Vladimir begins to find the long silences unendurable ('This is awful!') and in a fit of despair he has a vision of corpses in a charnel-house world (pp. 63–6). At nightfall he is restless and in pain; and Estragon is filled with the ultimate dread of not knowing what to do ('What'll we do, what'll we do!', p. 71). Vladimir's hallucinations ('It's Godot! At last!') are getting wilder, while Estragon feels trapped in hell, with no exit. Again, the comedy – the games and improvisations – is counterpointed by the terror of nothing to do and nothing to think about. In this predicament, Estragon calls out to his companion: 'Do you think God sees me?'; staggering and brandishing his fists, he shouts words resembling the mass: 'God have pity on me!' The cycle of hope and despair – and the evening of waiting in the theatre – is about to run down when the second 'diversion' of Pozzo and Lucky brings ironic 'reinforcements', a fit occasion for Vladimir's pastiche ceremonial speech:

> We are no longer alone, waiting for the night, waiting for Godot, waiting for . . . waiting.
> (p. 77)

The celebration is mocked by the impact of the second Pozzo and Lucky action, which turns Estragon and Vladimir once more into stage spectators (and vaudeville actors) endlessly playing off, and playing against, Pozzo's cries of help.

Their offers to help peter out in chattering and clowning and in Vladimir's rhetoric ('Let us do something while we have the chance!'). In the midst of this farcical episode, Pozzo's revelation that he is blind and that Lucky is dumb, and his speech on time and the simultaneity of birth and death ('They give birth astride of the grave', p. 89) echo the tones of traditional tragedy. Vladimir in his 'waking sleep' speech seems to remember the 'astride of a grave' image as he speculates on a possibly infinite series of observers watching each other ('At me too someone is looking'). Both the Pozzo and the Vladimir speeches transform the action into a dream-like state and contribute to the experience of a 'timeless time' which is prevalent in the whole play.

The final movement turns on the second coming of the Boy as messenger. The repetition, with variations of the end of Act I, exploits the deeply rooted human interest in patterns of anticipation, return and disappointment. Once again there is a cumulative sense of anti-climax ('No, Sir' / 'Yes, Sir' / Mr Godot 'does nothing, Sir'; he has a white beard). Yet the slow cross-examination with its long silences creates a new encounter, and the news of *nothing* still sounds as if it were about *something* important. The suicide attempt is repeated too, with Estragon forgetting that he has pulled his trousers down – a broad vaudeville act placed riskily near the end. The ending parallels Act I, counterpointing 'Yes, let's go' (this time spoken by Estragon) with *they do not move*, and suggesting that repetition could be endless – an infinite series of action/non-action sequences.

The account just given of endless 'waiting' as a type of action (so hard for the Western mind to conceptualise even when it has been experienced) should serve as a basis for interpreting the play. Thus we should avoid those eager leaps of ideological interpretation that reduce the play at a premature stage of reception: Existentialist (Godot shows man lost in a world after the death of God); Marxist (only the alienation of a late capitalist society, coupled with the hysteria of the cold war, can have produced such a work, where man ceases to be a political animal); Freudian (Gogo represents the *id*, Didi the *ego*); Christian (the play is a parable on man's need for salvation). . . :

THEATRE AND STRUCTURE

Waiting for Godot has been termed an 'anti-play', in a highly questionable catch-phrase which underlines its reduced 'dramatic' qualities: its lack of plot and logical movement (from exposition through turning-point to catastrophe), its digressions, and so on. Even so, no one has suggested that the scenes of the play should be shuffled, that we should perform it starting from the middle, or the end . . . If such randomness sounds like nonsense, it can at least make us reflect on the play's peculiar tautness of design; how balanced and interlinked are its scenes (and its digressions) along the axis of the two acts, with repetition and variation, and its overall symmetry.

Waiting for Godot uses and parodies what we expect from drama and the theatre, playing on our expectations by changing and counterpointing them. Even the two-act structure, the repetition of two cycles – which a wit called 'nothing happens, twice' – exploits our expectation of a 'dramatic' curve of action, relentless movement towards the final goal – as we know it from realist drama and from several Shakespeare plays.

Much of the tension in waiting comes from audience expectations of a 'dramatic' pattern. The rise/fall is expected and is disappointed, and so is the fall/rise; what we then get is a wholly new pattern, appropriate to a new kind of tragicomedy. The repeated acts also underline the endless action-in-non-action cycles, suggesting an infinite series: the end of the play *could* be the beginning of a third act, leading on to a fourth and fifth act, and so *ad infinitum*. But the economy of the two-act structure does its work well enough – pointing to potential infinity. We might think of Vladimir and Estragon as turning with a revolving stage that brings them back – at the end of each act – to the place they started from. Their space-time is cyclic, and they cannot opt out of their slow revolutions any more than the actor can leave off a role, step off the revolving stage.

The broad scenic units of the play – the two appearances of Pozzo and Lucky (a climax in each act) and of the Boy (a possible turning-point) are so constructed as to underline the repetition. Many other lesser units of construction help to emphasise this circularity, notably Vladimir's round song about the dog at the opening of Act II, which could go on 'for ever'. At the same time, the characters are moving in a definite direction – they are moving onward, or in Pozzo's favourite monosyllable 'On'. Onward looks like downward; their ageing, their deterioration, their time-spinning, are all part of a run-down, towards their eventual end. That sense of time's inexorable movement – onward movement as we know it and fear it, through doing and wasting – is integrated into the cyclic structure. It is made felt through the emphasis on a performance: an occasion here and now that passes the time for the audience, and which must be brought to an end. Internal references to time (the retrospect to the young Estragon and Vladimir, for example, the time, fifty years ago, when they might have jumped off the Eiffel Tower with dignity) further underline our ordinary time-consciousness. The long line of a possible past and a possible future cuts across the rotation of time present, the action before us.

The empty stage itself is clearly a device to magnify theatricality. Beckett does not use the empty stage as fully and elaborately as Pirandello does in *Six Characters in Search of an Author* (1921), to exploit the painful tension between so-called 'illusion' and assumed 'reality'. In *Waiting for Godot* the main function of staging the stage itself, as the setting of the action, is to underline its emptiness – a space to be filled with words and images (a tree, the moon rising at the end of Act I). Nothing quite like that has ever been attempted, though neither Greek nor Elizabethan drama relied on stage props, and modern stage design (from Craig and Appia on) has increasingly used the stage as an 'empty space', for reconstructing space. Drawing attention to the stage has the further benefit of distancing the action from the audience and pointing to players, roles, contrived movements, speech-making, the perpetual rehearsal of an improvised text that gets fixed. Imagination creates everything 'out of airy *nothing*'. Jokes and jocular allusions keep the physical 'obviousness' of the stage continuously before the audience, starting from the quietly ironic insult to the public:

> *Estragon moves to the centre, halts with his back to auditorium.*
> **Estragon** Charming spot. (*He turns, advances to front, halts facing auditorium.*)
> Inspiring prospects. (*He turns to Vladimir.*) Let's go.
>
> (p. 13)

In the middle of the first Pozzo and Lucky episode, just at the point where Pozzo is speaking in his most histrionic manner, like a ham actor, Vladimir and Estragon as stage audience 'let on' that they are aware of the kind of spectacle they have been exposed to and trapped in:

Vladimir	Charming evening we're having.
Estragon	Unforgettable.
Vladimir	And it's not over.
Estragon	Apparently not.
Vladimir	It's only beginning.
Estragon	It's awful.
Vladimir	Worse than pantomime.
Estragon	The circus.
Vladimir	The music hall.
Estragon	The circus.

(p. 35)

The irony of this internal reference to 'what is going on here in the theatre' gives the audience the chance to reflect on its own 'charming evening', and the attendant risks of 'it' not yet being over, as the digressions multiply. The reference to pantomime (the French version has *spectacle*), music hall and circus, sharpens awareness of the circus clown antics of Vladimir and Estragon (whether or not performed on a circus-like stage, as it was at the Round House, in 1981), and the music-hall patter in their dialogue can be distinctly heard.

The inward-pointing theatre metaphors are intensified in Act II where the enclosed but 'spacious' space of the theatre is used as an analogy for a place without exit, hell. In a triumphant moment the sounds heard off-stage are taken to announce the coming of Godot 'at last': Vladimir calls out to Estragon and drags him towards the wings, on the right, but Estragon 'gets lost' through his exit; Vladimir runs to meet him on the extreme left, but Estragon re-enters on the right. It is then that he cries out 'I'm in hell', in a context that makes it clear that all the exits have been blocked:

> Vladimir   We're surrounded! (*Estragon makes a rush towards back.*)
> Imbecile! There's no way out there. (*He takes Estragon by the arm and drags him towards front.*) There! Not a soul in sight! Off you go. Quick! (*He pushes Estragon towards auditorium. Estragon recoils in horror.*) You won't? (*He contemplates auditorium.*) Well, I can understand that. Wait till I see. (*He reflects.*) Your only hope left is to disappear.
>
> (p. 74)

The analogy, between the panic-stricken person who does not know which way to turn in an all-enveloping 'hell' and the actor suffering from stage fright (wanting to use the back as exit, and the front too), is one of many fused tragicomic effects. The music-hall-type joke of commenting on the auditorium does not lessen the horror. The audience is supposed to be absent, yet, presumably, it is the thought of facing the audience that adds to Estragon's horror when facing the auditorium – a double theatrical joke.

Such overt pointers to the theatre are reinforced by the most visible kind of physical stage routines: the boot-games, the long hat-passing number, the conscious miming, play-acting and cursing, which have been summarised earlier in this chapter. These are the acts that owe most to the popular theatre, especially to the English music hall, and the double act of vaudeville ('Flanagan and Allen'), though Beckett was doubtless also influenced by the comedians of the silent film (especially Chaplin and Buster Keaton) and perhaps also by Laurel and Hardy. The source matters much less than the revitalised use of elements of farce and clowning in the serious theatre.

The 'tragicomedy' is so pervasive that it probably covers all the scenes of the play. The two failed suicide attempts are memorable examples, especially the second one ('You could hang on to my legs.' / 'And who'd hang on to mine?'), placed precariously near the end of the play; but it is carefully timed to sustain the 'tragicomic tone' right to the end. The Pozzo and Lucky scenes fuse not just the tragic and the comic, but also the melodramatic and the farcical, in rapidly shifting tones. The episode in Act II where Pozzo goes on shouting for help while Estragon and Vladimir ignore or debate the situation risks broad farce – with the cumulative falls, and the sporting commentary on who is up, who down – in a scene that must accommodate the tragic overtones of Pozzo's blindness and his despairing speech on time and universal darkness. Similarly, the violence of Lucky's role – the kicks and counter-kicks, the terror of his physical and spiritual enslavement, aphasia and breakdown of thought – are seamlessly integrated in a circus act, which ends with the seizing of that failed performer's hat. In Shakespeare there is either comic relief – the 'Hell-Porter' in *Macbeth* – or the comic release that comes from a happy ending in a potentially tragic pattern (*Measure for Measure* and *The Winter's Tale*). In Chekhov the causes of laughter and tears co-exist in a social and personal reality where collisions of the noble and the banal, of sudden death and creaking boots, are inevitable. By contrast, *Waiting for Godot* is tragicomic at every level, from the beginning to the end of the play; from first meeting to the final failed suicide attempt.

Finding the vision of the play in overall structure and theatricality is not to forget that Beckett is, above all, a master of words. But the language of *Waiting for Godot* probably makes more allusions to the theatre than any other Beckett play. The characters often interact through speech as their dialogue is counterpointed by movement, gesture, auditive and visual effects. It remains true that Beckett's verbal art springs from an extreme view of language: a severance of words from objects, a denial that language can either represent or express the world 'out there', coupled with a recurrent, hypnotic desire for words to cease – for silence. *Waiting for Godot* is a fully embodied play *despite* Beckett's known views on the failure of language, and the total isolation of the speaker, the human animal that secretes words. The total impact of the play is richer, more concrete and multi-vocal than might be expected from Beckett's virtual negation of art and language. As our reading has tried to show, Beckett's dramatic and verbal art embodies precise images of action and a far-reaching vision of human existence. The impact of the play has not weakened in over three decades and is likely to endure, as far as a contemporary can tell, for all time.

From Andrew K. Kennedy, *Samuel Beckett* (Cambridge, 1989), pp. 24–31, 42–6.

NOTES

[Andrew K. Kennedy's essay comes from his valuable introductory study of Samuel Beckett. It would not be unfair to see this book as representing the important and still-influential strain of 'liberal-humanist' criticism of Beckett. Robustly sceptical of the dominative ambitions of theory and criticism, such work typically aims to show how Beckett affirms the identity and value of the 'human' spirit through close and responsive analysis of the particularities of the drama. Although many of Kennedy's assumptions about the nature of art and human identity are subjected to critique in later essays, his account of the self-reflexiveness of *Waiting for Godot* also forms a bridge between traditional critical views of Beckett's work and more recent accounts informed by different theoretical approaches. Ed.]

1. Samuel Beckett, *Waiting for Godot*, 2nd edn (London, 1965), p. 12. All references, inserted parenthetically in the text, will be to this edition.

2

Ways of Waiting in 'Waiting for Godot'

JAMES L. CALDERWOOD

The perfect title of a literary work, one might expect, would be, as it is in Beckett's *Waiting for Godot*, a synecdoche, a particularly meaningful part from which the reader could infer the whole. With that in mind, I'd like to trace out some of the implications of Beckett's title. But first let me note a general curiosity about the titles of plays, one that Beckett exacerbates to paradox in his paradoxical work: the simple fact that as compared to those of poems and novels the titles of plays appear in a different mode from the play itself. They are written, not spoken, whereas poems and their titles are both written. A reader first looks into Keats's words 'On First Looking into Chapman's Homer' before he looks into the words of the poem that appears below it. The one leads naturally into the other, so naturally, indeed, that many titles of poems are simply the first phrases or lines of the poems themselves, as in Keats's 'I Stood Tip-Toe'. In this case the title is a synecdoche in fact as well as in figure, an actual part of the poem that stands for the whole and exists both outside and inside it. Such a title is not a verbal microcosm or illuminating abbreviation of the whole but merely a tautology serving as an identifying tag.

So it is when we read a play as a written text. But the case is significantly altered when the play is performed. Because the title now exists in a different mode from that of the play, it seems outside it. *Waiting for Godot* is unusual in this respect, however, insamuch as it attempts to incorporate its title into its performance, and to do so in a manner that renders it elusively significant. In the first place, the title is within the play quite literally by virtue of its appearance at the end of Gogo and Didi's oft-repeated verbal routine:

Let's go.
We can't.
Why not?
We're waiting for Godot.[1]

But it is also within the play more complexly. If we adopt the view that one of the things *Waiting for Godot* waits for is its own summarising title, then the title is a concluding continuation of the play. That is, the title precedes the play, and yet as a synecdoche it does not begin but end it, since not until the whole has become whole can a synecdoche represent it. The apparent ending of the play is merely a state of incompletion, a still-waiting:

Vladimir   Well? Shall we go?
Estragon   Yet, let's go.
   They do not move.
(p. 87)

Their failure to move inevitably forces us as audience to take up and complete their familiar verbal routine: 'We can't ... Why not? ... We're waiting for Godot.' And that takes us back to the play's title, which, though suggested by the ending of the play, resides outside it, in the voice of our imagination. Thus we encounter a title directly opposite to Keats's 'I Stood Tip-Toe', in that it trails the last line of the work instead of preceding the first. From this standpoint the play waits for the title that will complete it.

To complicate matters, we could take the opposite and more commonsense view, that the title waits for the play that will complete it. That is, we could argue that the title appropriately precedes the play because that is how the play was written. Beckett had a vague notion about a play whose main action was waiting for someone named Godot; he sketched out this idea in the words *Waiting for Godot*; and he then filled in the details by writing the play. Instead of the last lines of the play pointing to an apparently conclusive title, the title points forward to the play about to begin.

But of course, Beckett being Beckett, he would not want it one way or the other when it could be both at once. In that case the title and the text form a circle, like the synecdochic 'round' with which Didi begins Act II:

> A dog came in the kitchen
> And stole a crust of bread.
> Then cook up with a ladle
> And beat him till he was dead.
>
> Then all the dogs came running
> And dug the dog a tomb –
>
> (*He stops, broods, resumes.*)
>
> Then all the dogs came running
> And dug the dog a tomb
> And wrote upon the tombstone
> For the eyes of dogs to come:
>
> A dog came in the kitchen . . .
> (p. 52)

The round has neither a beginning nor an ending, merely a brooding pause whenever Didi reaches the word 'tomb'. At that point the dog in the song passes from life to death, and Didi's song about a dog killed by a cook becomes a song written by dogs on a tombstone telling about a dog killed by a cook and the arrival of another pack of dogs who write upon another tombstone a song about a dog killed by a cook . . . and so on. The process is simultaneously recursive (Didi's originating song is on hold until the tomb-songs have concluded), infinitely linear (from tombstone to tombstone), and self-containedly cyclical (each song returning to the first). Moreover, the tomb-songs seem Escher-fashion to be outside Didi's song and yet inside it too – each inscribed (not sung) on a different tombstone, yet each a repetitious furtherance of the original song.

If Didi's circular song is like Beckett's play,[2] his brooding pause at the moment when the dog is about to be interred is like Beckett's elusive title, which marks a pause at the moment when his 'dead' play is about to be interred in the theatre. But if the ending of the play is in one sense a theatrical death and entombment, it's also, as we've seen, a preface to resumption. Thus the play un-ends on the not-going of Didi and Gogo, a not-going that leads into the summarising title *Waiting for Godot* and hence back to the beginning of the play where the words 'Nothing to be done' (written, as it were, on its tombstone) confirm the undone-ness of its ending. The play, like the round, has neither beginning nor end; the title merely marks a pause, like Didi's, at the point of the play's daily theatrical demise, the fall of the curtain, prior to its resuscitation in tomorrow's performance. If the title is a tautology, it is properly so, since the play is a circular tautology that ends where it begins, with two characters, Didi and Gogo, whose names end where they begin.

WAITING AS ERASURE

The paradoxes of Beckett's title extend beyond its location to include its grammar. Is 'waiting' a verb or a noun, or more precisely a present participle or a gerund? Does it imply something like 'Gogo and Didi are *Waiting for Godot*' or, rather, '*Waiting for Godot* is what Gogo and Didi are doing'? In the latter case, as gerund, 'waiting' assumes the substantiality of a noun, an objectlike status as a completed action, as in 'The Wait for Godot'. However, as a participle, it suggests the ongoingness of a verbal action, as in 'We are Waiting for Godot'. As it is, suspended between noun and verb, 'waiting' waits in a state of incompleteness for its grammatical identity to be established – (the taxonomic tragicomedy of 'waiting'!). Thus its grammatical ambiguity as noun-verb coalesces with its semantic ambiguity as a form of unmoving movement or inactive action and reflects the larger tendency of the play toward the spatial arrest of form and the temporal flow of performance.

This leads us to the negativity of waiting. As an instance of *ekphrasis* 'waiting' exhibits self-negating impulses in which the spatial seeks to cancel the temporal and vice versa.[3] Moreover, as an activity, waiting is negative by virtue of having no fixed identity and hence of being impossible to recognise. Of course like eating, talking, or jumping, it can be defined in words. The dictionary defines jumping, for instance, as 'To spring clear of the ground by muscular effort', and it defines waiting as 'To hold oneself ready for an arrival or an occurrence'. But if you ask me how I know someone is jumping, I need only point and say 'Well, that's what she's doing – flexing her knees, gathering herself, and springing into the air'. However, if the same question is asked about waiting, I will be at a loss for an adequate ostensive definition. Jumping is a physical activity, but waiting is – well, what is it? If I point to a man sitting on a bench at a bus stop and say 'He's waiting', you will think waiting means sitting on a bench – or whittling or break dancing or throwing sticks for a dog. I am repeatedly obliged to say 'No, that's not it. It's not what he's doing but what he's not doing that constitutes waiting'.

So waiting, which implies the absence of the waited-for, is itself mysteriously absent. Moreover, waiting is a self-erasing non-activity, since it negates the transient activities we engage in while waiting. Jumping, whittling, reading, even staring in annoyance at our watch – whatever we're doing is nullified by virtue of our waiting. Although these activities are undeniably occurring, they are rendered parenthetical to what we are 'really' doing – i.e. waiting.[4] Thus Gogo and Didi struggle with their boots and their hats, engage in greeting ceremonies, ponder the mysteries of the Crucifixion and the enigmas of suicide, eat carrots and turnips, talk with Pozzo and listen to Lucky, but they always come back to the nullifying words:

> Let's go.
> We can't.
> Why not?
> We're waiting for Godot.

These negative aspects of waiting have disconcerting implications for our experience of the play in the theatre, but in keeping with our subject let us defer that issue to a later time, meanwhile taking a glance at time itself.

WAITING AND TIME

The overriding importance of waiting nullifies not only what we are doing but also the time in which we are doing it. Not all time: waiting erases the past and diminishes the present but apparently aggrandises the future in which the waited-for will appear. Or will it? To wait for the future is to wait also for the unknown, and thus to put oneself at risk. Even to wait for the dawn is to give hostages to the solar system, yielding the security of the present for that which, in times fearful of Apocalypse – that is, in all times – may never come. When Didi says 'We are not saints, but we have kept our appointment. How many people can boast as much?' Gogo deflates him by saying 'Billions' (p. 73). But the fact that they have kept their appointment lends both merit and desperation to their waiting. That is, in a mutable world appointments, vows, contracts, promises, and so forth are attempts to control time and give shape to one's life, to escape the uncertainties of an unknowable future. However, the fact that the two tramps have kept their end of the bargain without Godot putting in an appearance implies that in their world time refuses to be shaped. Thus it is rather heroically pathetic that they wait for a future that has failed them (as they might say) if not once, always. Ultimately, keeping their appointment suggests merely their having been born along with billions of others into a world where all appointments have the character of one hand clapping.

In *Waiting for Godot* the past is no more secure or knowable than the future. When Beckett begins Act II with the 'round' about the cook and the dog, he implicitly raises the question of how the past is preserved in the present. Tombstones are one traditional form of preservation, but as Sir Thomas Browne lamented, 'Tombstones tell truth scarce thirty years'. Nevertheless, the tombstones of the dogs preserve the past perfectly. Indeed, once we are 'beyond' Didi's voiced song, each of the inscribed tomb-songs so perfectly repro-duces its predecessors that past and present cannot be distinguished. A situation very like that in the play, where each day is identical to the last, each night's beating is indistinguishable from the others, and even carrots and turnips are hard to tell apart. *Waiting for Godot* itself, as Vivian Mercier wittily put it, is a play in which nothing happens – twice.

Yet the play is clearly less repetitious than the tomb-songs or Didi's and Gogo's names: in Act II the tree has 'four or five leaves', Pozzo and Lucky have fallen on harder times, and, to be sure, a song about a dog and a cook is introduced. 'Things have changed here since yesterday' Didi shrewdly notes, and Gogo unintentionally replies 'Everything oozes'. Still, how to know if things have changed or not? How to know what they have changed from? 'Yesterday' is Didi's point of departure, and during much of Act II he unwinds yesterday as an Ariadne's thread into the labyrinth of today. But yesterday is as uncertain as Gogo's memory, which is sketchy at best ('I'm not a historian' [p. 60]), and Pozzo's which is non-existent. Only the audience remembers clearly, which means that Act II is a radically different experience for us than Act I, because now we know that Godot will not come. The Boy came at the end of Act I but not Godot. He or a different Boy may come at the end of Act II but not Godot. Things change and stay the same; as Gogo observes in a Heraclitean mood, 'It's never the same pus from one second to the next' (p. 55). His and Didi's routines may differ, but one thing is constant: they are waiting for Godot. And as we have seen, waiting negates little differences anyhow, leaving only the big difference, the absence of Godot.

The absences and uncertainties of memory on the characters' parts would seem to suggest that they live almost entirely in the present. But what is the present without the past and the future? Its home is the temporal space between the 'no longer' and the 'not yet'. But for Gogo and Didi the present exists merely as an unbearable route to a future in which Godot's arrival will justify their present waiting. If he comes. But he won't. The past is lost to memory, the future is not yet and never to be, and the present is negated. From one standpoint – the felt presence of duration – there is a dreadful excess of time in *Godot*. From another – the erasure of past, present, and future – there is no time at all in it. Time in this timeless play is simultaneously present and absent.[5]

WAITING AS TRAVELLING

A country road. A tree. Evening. 'The road', Pozzo says, 'is free to all . . . It's a disgrace. But there you are' (p. 23). There too are Gogo and Didi, quite literally 'on the road'. Whatever they once were, they are tramps now, which means that like all tramps they are in a perpetual state of unfulfilment, their lives defined by what they lack – money, food, clothes, shelter, booze, family, friends, work, respect, security, and so on. According to the myth of tramp-life, tramps move down the road or the tracks in endless pursuit of an elusive destination which is figured in folk song as the paradisal Big Rock Candy Mountain where:

> the cops have wooden legs,
> The bulldogs all have rubber teeth
> And the hens lay soft-boiled eggs.

But the Big Rock Candy Mountain is not on the service station maps, nor does an authentic tramp want it to be. For the trampish mode of travel is an end in itself, not, like that of the businessman, a means to a destination. The road Gogo and Didi are 'on' does not lead toward a destination, it *is* their destination.

For Pozzo, the capitalist possessor of goods and one sorry carrier of goods, things are different. When he first appears he announces that he is travelling for a purpose, to sell Lucky at the fair (p. 30). For him travelling is a moving form of waiting – waiting for the fair –

and, as waiting, it is self-nullifying. Purely functional, a means not an end, such travel is merely a spatial parenthesis between departure and destination. Thus it's understandable that when the blind Pozzo encounters Didi and Gogo in Act II he can't remember their previous meeting, his intention to sell Lucky, Lucky's dancing and thinking, his own sightedness (p. 8). Inbetweenness doesn't register with him. By this time, however, there is no inbetweenness for Pozzo; he no longer has a destination. He's become like the tramp who makes travelling an end in itself. He cannot stay, his business is going ('On!') – going and, to be sure, falling, then going again. This entails another of Beckett's paradoxes: if travel is an end in itself, then you can never arrive at a destination because you are already there.

Pozzo's endless going is the opposite of Didi and Gogo's endless staying. Yet going or staying, there's no escape from the human plight. Whereas Pozzo's purposive travel toward an end, the fair, becomes on his return journey a pointless end in itself, Didi and Gogo's pointless travel of the past has now apparently become a purposive waiting for the future. However, if waiting is a means to an end, it is a very curious means, since it can do nothing to bring about the desired meeting, whereas travelling is instrumental; it gets you there. By travelling faster you can reduce the time you have to wait before reaching your destination, but how do you wait faster or more efficiently? The only way to speed up waiting is by trying to forget you are doing it. Explore inside your boot for pebbles, have a little canter with words, 'do the tree', eat a carrot, curse each other, or simply give it all up and say 'Let's go . . .'. And you're back where you were. And even if you could go, if the road were a means to a destination and not the destination itself, look at Pozzo and Lucky. That's how it is on this bitch of an earth in this bitch of a play.

. . . FOR GODOT

The part of the play's title I have omitted to this point is the part the play omits, *Godot*. How to account for that? All attempts to establish Godot's identity encounter Beckett's insistence that if he had known he would have said – which of course may or may not be true. At any rate, God, Godin, the millennium, death, salvation, Judgement Day – the slate of candidates is as endless as waiting. Perhaps Beckett's anti-allegorical bent should warn us against thinking too precisely on the matter. Surely we are safer in saying what

Godot is not than in saying what he is. One clue to his non-identity lies in Beckett's figuring the tramps' painful waiting as a slow crucifixion. Though Gogo says 'All my life I've compared myself to him' (p. 49), the interpretive point, surely, is not to associate Didi and Gogo presumptuously with Christ but rather with the two thieves who shared his agony. Since one thief was damned and the other saved, we could argue that what Didi and Gogo await is neither damnation nor salvation but merely an outcome, an 'end-game'. Let Godot come in whatever form he likes – God, Pozzo, or The Great Carrot – as long as he puts an end to waiting.

As the play goes on, however, Godot disappears even as the possibility of an indefinable outcome. Waiting now becomes a pointless habit, as Didi implies when Pozzo and Lucky stumble upon the scene in Act II: 'We are no longer alone, waiting for the night, waiting for Godot, waiting for . . . waiting' (p. 71). Instead of waiting-for we have merely waiting. The past has faded with fading memories, now the future fades as well. Without them the present is everything and yet nothing, just as without the waited-for, without Godot, waiting itself is everything and yet nothing. As a self-nullifying activity, waiting erases itself. Now, with the possibility of Godot also erased, the title of the play seems in danger of being reduced to *Waiting*. . . .

Still, since we can count no man happy until he has speculated about the meaning of 'Godot', let me offer my own exercise in divination by pointing out that Godot read backwards is 'Tod-dog' if we let the 'd' do double duty, hence 'death-dog', which reminds us of the round about the dog in the kitchen killed by the cook and memorialised on tombstones. However, 'Dog' is of course 'God' spelled backwards, and so if we reverse the name to 'Tod-dog' and read from left to right we get 'death-dog' and if we read from right to left we get 'god-death'. Thus death and god meet at the centre of the name for which the tramps are waiting, just as death and the dog meet within the song Didi sings, and as death and birth meet in Pozzo's arresting metaphor 'They give birth astride of a grave'. We have a Joycean word, then, in which 'death', 'dog', and 'god' combine. We might argue that since 'God' is by definition immortal, he can die only in his earthly inverted form as 'dog'. Dogs die but God lives on, if only in the hopes of two tramps. For that matter, even the dog has a kind of immortality in the endlessness of the song: death transcended by art. Art keeps the dog alive that life would otherwise kill and forget. And just as the dog exists in a curious state of life-in-death, so God exists as an undying possibility just beyond the tramps' reach despite being killed in their hopes each day. In a larger sense, as the song keeps the dog alive, so Beckett's play, the implication runs, keeps God alive despite his meeting 'death' within his own name. In fact, when 'God' and 'death' cohabit within a name, when they verbally collide without destroying each other, both are rendered subordinate to, contained by language, as everyone within the text of the play is. The truth of God, the truth of death are unimportant. Does God exist (as a white-bearded old man)? No matter, he exists in language, in theology; words keep him alive, whatever his ontological status. Is death merely death, a terminus, or is it, as in the name 'Godot' turned backwards, an avenue to God? Or are God and death counter-forces held in suspension by language? It's not the truth of these things that matters, Beckett suggests; it's the language, the style, the rightness of the words in which the truth(less) is couched. 'I am interested', Beckett said, 'in the shape of ideas even if I do not believe in them . . . It is the shape that matters.'[6]

WAITING AS THEATRE

In choosing his title as he has, Beckett reveals a delight in paradox that puts the mode of existence of his play in question and confuses our theatrical experience with our experiences both before and after the performance.[7] Most plays have designs on our post-theatrical lives. They will seek to galvanise us into political and social awareness in Brecht's epic theatre or to purge us in Artaud's theatre of cruelty, or in some manner to teach us and delight us and send us on our way the better for what we have thought and felt. Beckett is not above delighting us. If Gogo and Didi make a kind of art of waiting, Beckett most surely makes an art of *Waiting for Godot*, an art grounded in negation. In keeping with his remark giving priority to the shape over the content of ideas, Beckett expresses the chaotic emptiness of life in a play that is scrupulously crafted and formed, and proclaims the meaninglessness of language in passages of arresting eloquence and beauty. He makes a music hall aria of despair and a *lazzo* of spiritual distress. It's the shape that matters, and Beckett makes lovely shapes.

But all this song, slapstick, verbal pattern, and rounded form – the artful shapes of play within the play – is self-negating. The play

places its own presence and our experience of it 'under erasure'.[8]
Moreover, as I've suggested, it puts under erasure our experience
before and after it as well. Take the 'before' first. We have come to
the theatre for what we regard as the climax of our day, a
performance of the new and much-talked-about play by Samuel
Beckett. We have waited for *Waiting for Godot*, and now as the
curtain rises on the two tramps the appointment has been kept;
Waiting for Godot has come. But then Gogo ceases wrestling with
his boot and says 'Nothing to be done'. And as this 'nothing doing'
continues in various forms we gradually realise that we have not
ceased waiting, for the play's coming is a curious deferral of coming.
Thus our theatrical experience is merely a continuation of the
waiting we have experienced before coming to the play. Moreover, if
we have been waiting all day for the performance, then what we have
done all day — work, play, whittle, jump — is negated in the same
manner that Gogo and Didi's stage foolery is negated by the
underlying fact of their waiting.

Thus the play is an unarriving Godot to its tramplike audience.
However, the reverse is equally true: the audience is an unarriving
Godot to the tramp-like play. The play, after all, has waited for the
audience as much as the audience has waited for the play, and now
here the audience is. Or is it? When Gogo, thinking Godot has come,
rushes madly about seeking an escape, Didi drags him to the front of
the stage and cries:

> There! Not a soul in sight! Off you go! Quick! (*He pushes Estragon
> towards auditorium. Estragon recoils in horror.*) You won't? (*He
> contemplates auditorium.*) Well, I can understand that. Wait till I see.
> (*He reflects.*) Your only hope left is to disappear.
>
> (p. 68)

Didi's 'Not a soul in sight!' honours the stage convention of realistic
theatre that the presence of the audience must not be acknowledged,
but it honours it by acknowledging the presence of the audience. It is
precisely what Shakespeare has Falstaff do when, just before stab-
bing the dead Hotspur, he looks about the theatre and says 'Nothing
confutes me but eyes, and nobody sees me' (*I Henry IV*, V.v. 128). In
both instances the effect is to render the audience present by asserting
its absence — the audience is negated into being.

Since things are defined by what they are not, we may draw on that
binary opposition structuralists are so fond of and observe that in the
semiology of theatre the play on stage is not the audience, and the

audience is not the play on stage. But precisely for that reason each needs the other to tell it what it is (not). Without the audience the play is not a play, only a series of empty gestures and unaddressed speeches; it acquires a pathetic half-being very much like Gogo and Didi without Godot (or like the humiliated players in *Rosencrantz and Guildenstern are Dead* when they discover that the anti-heroes have walked away and left them performing before no one [Act II]). And by the same token, without a play to see and hear, an audience dissolves into a meaningless assemblage of individuals.

But this needs refining, since it's not really the 'play' that waits for the audience or the audience that waits for the play. Rather, the actors and the stage wait for the audience that waits for them. When the two parties keep their appointment in the theatre the result is the arrival of 'Godot' – that is, what we think of as 'the play'. In this theatrical potluck meal the actors bring part of the play with them – dialogue, costumes, gestures – and the audience brings part of it with them, in their willing imaginations. When the two meet the play apparently arrives, and for the space of a couple of hours the actors are (and are not) the characters they play, and the stage is (and is not) a country road with a tree at evening. During the performance we may feel that we are experiencing the Godot of theatrical fulfilment, the play we have all waited for. But of course it is not really the play that has arrived, only a performance of it. The play itself, whatever that may be, hides somewhere behind its various performances, a Kantian noumenon. Like Godot, it will never come, and it will be here again tomorrow.

WAITING FOR MEANING

As we have seen, the play is a baffling combination of presence and absence. It is there before us on stage, being acted out, so it must be present. Yet the action of the play is waiting, and waiting cannot be dramatised. What is present, then, is not waiting but only the irrelevancies Gogo and Didi engage in while waiting, the shaped foolery with which Beckett beguiles our passing of the time. Thus the periodic cry of the tramps, 'Let's go, we can't, why not, we're waiting for Godot', issues from the audience as well. We as much as they have come here full of expectation, counting on seeing a play in which the transient confusions of the present would be clarified in the future, a play that would complete patterns, supply meanings, fashion a form, provide a closure. Form itself, as Kenneth Burke has put it, consists in the arousal and satisfaction of expectations in the audience.[9] In these terms Beckett's play is indeed formed, but in such a way as to make frustration satisfying. Thus it leads us to expect that Godot will not come, and then it presents us with Godot's climactic not-coming. Beckett dangles a turnip before our noses that tastes, alas, wonderfully like a turnip.

When the play is over we are no longer left waiting for it. Free at last! But of course what the play has forced upon us is the realisation that not merely our time in the theatre but our lives themselves are consumed in waiting for a Godot who will never come. Death will come but not Godot. Meanwhile we eat carrots on good days and turnips on bad ones, complain of our kidneys and our feet, contradict one another, get annoyed with one another, cling to one another, test the strength of tree limbs and belts, reason like Lucky, own and domineer and ultimately fall down like Pozzo, go to plays by Samuel Beckett, write about them, read what has been written about them, and wait. Still, if the play has made us realise this, then its meaning is not wholly deferred. Godot has come, after all – to tell us he will not come. It is Beckett's version of the hermeneutic circle. Every statement proclaiming the death of meaning exempts itself.

Still, Beckett doesn't actually proclaim the death of meaning. He says 'We are waiting for meaning'. Meaning is not yet. Is that more hopeful? Not if it entails a waiting like that of Gogo and Didi. If meaning is not yet, then when? Not at the end of the play. The play is not a periodic sentence whose final word we await to know what has been said. It is more like Lucky's thought-speech, which 'ends' with the word 'unfinished' (p. 42) – the verbal equivalent to the play's terminal 'Let's go' followed by *They do not move*. It is also the verbal opposite to Christ's 'It is finished', uttered back in the days of quick crucifixions when things had an end, even plays perhaps. But when things go on and on, when there is no defining outcome, no end, then it's not what is said or done that counts but the style in which it is said or done. When Gogo insists he wasn't doing anything, Didi replies: 'Perhaps you weren't. But it's the way of doing it that counts, the way of doing it, if you want to go on living' (p. 54). Style, form, shape, these matter. In fact they not only matter; they may *be* the matter – the meaning. Thus at the end, when we expect meaning to crystallise and a closure to take place, the play passes on, with a brooding pause at the title, to the incipient form and meaning of its (non)opening. It is not that the play is without meaning, only that its meanings are contained by its own cyclical form. Its meaning is unending – which suggests an infinity of unfolding signification – but it is also, like Godot, 'not yet'.[10]

This suggests that the play is by no means a naïve nihilistic denial of meaning but rather a demonstration that meaning is elusively embedded within the play itself. Beckett doesn't merely say 'Meaning is not yet' but rather with the smirk of a Cretan 'The assertion "Meaning is not yet" has meaning'. It is like Gogo and Didi's efforts to pass the time. In the light of Godot's future presence, they mean nothing; in the light of his present absence, they mean everything. So they give waiting a presence that waiting negates, and Beckett gives his play, and our lives, a meaning that their unmeaning denies.

What have I said? Let's go.

From *Modern Drama*, 29 (1986), 363–75.

NOTES

[James L. Calderwood's essay first appeared in the influential journal *Modern Drama*, and is included here as one of a number of essays exemplifying different forms of deconstructive readings of Beckett's drama. Its account of the nature of waiting in *Waiting for Godot* makes paradoxically actual the experience of the dissolution of actuality which the play embodies. Like other essays in this volume, it demonstrates plainly that deconstructive criticism entails not the aggressive and once-and-for-all liquidation of the coherence possessed by a given text, but a faithfully attentive discussion of the ways in which a text can simultaneously establish and undermine its own 'truth'. Ed.]

1. This routine first occurs on p. 14 of the text as printed in *Samuel Beckett: Complete Dramatic Works* (London, 1986). All references will be to this edition and incorporated parenthetically in the text.

2. With regard to the dog-song – and for that matter to the notion of paradox in general in the play – see Yasuhiro Ogawa, '*Waiting for Godot*' or the Texture of Paradox', *The Northern Review*, 11 (Japan), 13–36. Professor Ogawa notes that 'In addition to its circular or, more correctly, Chinese box fabric ... the song reflects upon the play's plot and as such can be understood as a metadramatic device commenting upon the whole play' (25).

3. See Murray Krieger, 'The Ekphrastic Principle and the Still Movement of Poetry: or *Laokoon* Revisited', in *The Play and Place of Criticism*

(Baltimore, 1967), pp. 105–28. By 'ekphrastic' Krieger means the spatial-temporal 'ever-never' aspect of art, its tendency simultaneously to seek arrest and continuance.

4. As Bert O. States observes, 'Yet it is often pointed out that the French title, *En attendant Godot*, puts the emphasis squarely where it belongs (and where the English title does not): on the interim rather than on the expectation; not the act of waiting *for* something but the activity of waiting itself' *(The Shape of Paradox: An Essay on 'Waiting for Godot'* [Berkeley and Los Angeles, 1978], p. 49). The French title only makes more obviously ironic the point I'm urging, that 'the activity of waiting itself' is precisely what cannot be dramatised.

5. Almost everyone has had a say about time in *Godot*, perhaps most notably Richard Schechner, 'There's Lots of Time in *Godot*', *Modern Drama*, 9 (1966), 268–76.

6. Cited by Bert O. States – whose own book takes up the subject of how shape matters and how matter is shaped in the play (see note 3 above) – as appearing first in Harold Hobson's 'Samuel Beckett, Dramatist of the Year', *International Theatre Annual*, no. 1 (London, 1956), pp. 153–5.

7. In speaking about the 'art of playing' in *Godot* I should mention the comprehensive and consistently insightful treatment of the play from a theatrical standpoint by Sidney Homan in his *Beckett's Theaters: Interpretations for Performance* (Lewisburg, 1984).

8. By 'under erasure' here I refer of course to the Heideggerian and Derridean practice of crossing out a word and letting the deletion stand, to indicate a concept that is invalid but necessary, that both 'is' and 'is not'. It seems clear that in some respects Beckett has anticipated Derrida's notions of erasure, dissemination, supplementation, *différance* and the general view that nothing is ever simply present or absent.

9. Kenneth Burke, 'Psychology and Form', in *Counter-Statement* (New York, 1931).

10. Thus if we think of the play as a complex set of signifiers in search of a signified called Godot, then it is clear that like the dog-song it can never escape from its own endless chain of signification. As when we hunt for the meaning of a word in the dictionary or in our heads, only to discover more words – signifiers seeking signifieds that turn out to be simply other signifiers – so the play rejects the possibility of a transcendental signified outside the field of discourse. By 'transcendental signified' I refer of course to Jacques Derrida's contention that discourse is 'a system in which the central signified, the original or transcendental signified, is never absolutely present outside a system of differences'. As he goes on to say, 'The absence of the transcendental signified extends the domain and the play of signification infinitely' ('Structure, Sign, and Play', in *Writing and Difference*, trans. Alan Bass [London, 1978], p. 280).

3

Samuel Beckett and the Postmodern: Language Games, Play and 'Waiting for Godot'

JEFFREY NEALON

In Samuel Beckett's *Waiting for Godot*, Vladimir and Estragon pass the time while waiting by playing at a series of games – language games – which constitute their existence and form their social bond. Language games and play are two key concepts in much of contemporary thought; as Wittgenstein – the 'father' of language-game theory – writes, 'the term "language game" is meant to bring into prominence the fact that the *speaking* of a language is part of an activity, a form of life (*Lebensform*)'.[1] As Wittgenstein sees it, a word is analogous to a chess piece, and utterances can be thought of as moves within the language games that make up the human social bond. This notion of language games, as appropriated from Wittgenstein and modified by subsequent thinkers, has had a great influence on contemporary thinking about language, shifting the emphasis of language analysis from an enquiry into the meaning of a statement to its role in a language game. As Fredric Jameson writes in his foreword to Jean-François Lyotard's *The Postmodern Condition*:

> ... utterances are now seen less as a process of transmission of information or messages, or in terms of some network of signs or even

signifying systems, than as . . . the 'taking of tricks', the trumping of a communicational adversary, an essentially conflictual relationship between tricksters.[2]

Such, it seems to me, is the state of language games in *Godot*; it is the play of Vladimir and Estragon's words, not any agreed-upon meaning for them, which constitutes their social bond. Waiting for legitimation of their society in Godot is, from the beginning, unnecessary; they constitute a society which is always already formed by their participation in language games. As Lyotard writes:

> . . . there is no need to resort to some fiction of social origins to establish that language games are the minimum relation required for society to exist . . . the question of the social bond, insofar as it is a question, is itself a language game, the game of inquiry. It immediately positions the person who asks, as well as the addressee and the referent asked about: it is *already* the social bond.
>
> (p. 15)

This postmodern social bond is suspended in *Godot* by Vladimir and Estragon's drive to recuperate a transcendent principle – represented by Godot – which they feel will give meaning to their lives and their speech, thereby legitimating their society. All their games have reference to one metagame (or what Lyotard, in his discussion of modernism, calls a 'grand Narrative'): waiting for Godot. Theirs is the discourse of modernism, which 'legitimates itself with reference to a metadiscourse . . . making an explicit appeal to some grand narrative' (p. xxiii), some recuperative metaphysical system such as Platonism, the Christian God, the Hegelian dialectic of spirit, transcendent subjectivity, or the hermeneutics of meaning. These grand narratives, upon which modernism bases itself, have all broken down, giving way to a postmodern society which is characterised by incredulity toward both metanarratives and legitimation in them. In postmodern society, it is precisely in the social bond of language and language games that we can legitimate our own society. In such a postmodern society, people have untied themselves from the belief in a metaphysical, trans-historical, absolute ground for their existence. It has become apparent that no such system exists, but this does not reduce postmodern society to barbarity and chaos, as the modernists thought it would. Postmoderns look to themselves and their communicational interaction in society to legitimate their existence.

In *Waiting for Godot*, Gogo and Didi *have* such a communicational society but they do not realise it because of their deep-seated drive toward legitimation in Godot. Early in the play we see how this belief in a static metaphysical support displaces any postmodern notion of society:

> Estragon   Let's go.
> Vladimir   We can't.
> Estragon   Why not?
> Vladimir   We're waiting for Godot.[3]

This simple sequence occurs several times throughout the play,[4] and always after a long pause following the final 'trick' played in a language game: when their games break down or are played out, they constantly refer back to their metagame, their metadiscourse – Godot. For example, after Pozzo and Lucky leave near the end of the first act, we have this exchange:

> Pozzo . . . Adieu.
> *Long silence*
> Vladimir   That passed the time.
> Estragon   It would have passed in any case.
> Vladimir   Yes, but not so rapidly.
> *Pause*
> Estragon   What do we do now?
> Vladimir   I don't know.
> Estragon   Let's go.
> Vladimir   We can't.
> Estragon   Why not?
> Vladimir   We're waiting for Godot.
>
> (p. 31)

For Vladimir and Estragon, the grand Narrative of Godot imposes a rigid metaphysical limit on their gaming. To suggest these limits, Beckett employs a spatial metaphor: Vladimir and Estragon cannot *go* anywhere (disrupt the limits of their gaming) because they have inscribed themselves within the limits of one static, universal metagame, to which they constantly return when their smaller games have run their course. They play comfortably within these limits, but never attempt to transgress or disrupt them; in short, they play modern language games, not postmodern ones.

In postmodern language games, the limits of the game are not given from outside the game, but rather, as Lyotard writes, 'the limits themselves are the stakes and provisional results of language strategies' (p. 17). In postmodern language games, the goal of the game is to make moves which expand the limits of the game, constantly disrupting its margins. This disruption and expansion of the limits of language games allow for a corresponding expansion of what can be thought; since we think in language, the de-limitation of an existing language game allows for inventive, creative thought. As Paul Feyerabend writes, 'without a constant misuse of language there cannot be any discovery, any progress'.[5] To take a relatively simple example, non-Euclidean geometry could not have been 'invented' if someone had not transgressed and disrupted the limits of the language game we call plane geometry. If mathematicians of the early twentieth century had believed – as mathematicians and philosophers from Euclid's time to the late nineteenth century did – that Euclidean plane geometry was an absolute, they would not have been able to think beyond its limits and posit a non-Euclidean geometry. Such a disruption of the ruling order – or, in Feyerabend's terms, such a 'misuse of language' – is always paralogistic respective to the ruling paradigm because it seeks to disrupt this model by which it will be judged. A mathematician cannot *think* three-dimensional geometry if she feels that plane geometry is an absolute; it simply would not make sense relative to the ruling paradigm. So, unlike modern gaming, this disruption of limits – this postmodern gaming – does not simply reinforce and recuperate the grand Narratives of the past; rather, it refines and reinforces our abilities to think at, against, and beyond the stifling limits of previous thought. In Lyotard's conception of postmodern language games, 'invention is always born of dissension' (p. xxv).

In *Waiting for Godot*, the best example of this dissension and movement at the margins of a language game is the speech that is perhaps the key to the entire play: Lucky's 'think', which can be seen as a transgression and disruption of the limits of the ultimate metagame – Western metaphysics, the language game of truth. The text of Lucky's speech is akin to the product of taking all the great works of Western thought, putting them through a paper shredder, and pasting them back together at random. Beckett directs Lucky's long monologue against the popular notion that philosophy's job is to restore unity to man's learning, a job which philosophers can only do by recuperating some metanarrative which links together all moments in human history within a single, continuous metaphysical system. Lucky's think, though, is a narrative that disrupts and deconstructs all notions of universal, ahistorical, consistent metanarrative – all Godots. He begins:

> Given the existence as uttered forth in the public works of Puncher
> and Wattmann of a personal God *quaquaquaqua* with a white beard
> *quaquaquaqua outside time* without extension who from the heights
> of divine apathia divine athambia divine aphasia loves us dearly with
> some exceptions *for reasons unknown but time will tell* and suffers
> like the divine Miranda with those who *for reasons unknown but time
> will tell* are plunged in torment plunged in fire whose fire flames if that
> continues and who can doubt it will fire the firmament that is to say
> blast hell to heaven so blue and still and calm so calm with a *calm
> which even though intermittent is better than nothing* . . .
>
> (p. 28, my emphasis)

Lucky's think is directed against all the grand Narratives of Western
metaphysics, which ground themselves in discourse claiming to be:
referential and self-validating ('quaquaquaqua'); ahistorical ('outside
time'); metaphysical or mystical ('for reasons unknown'); teleological and revelatory ('but time will tell'); and bulwarks against
radical scepticism ('a calm which even though intermittent is better
than nothing').

Lucky's think exposes the limits imposed by all prior objectivist
thinking; it is a thoroughly postmodern language game that moves at
the limit of what has been thought. It is a speech of liberation set
against the metaphysical tyranny of limitations on thought imposed
by limitations on language. A clear example of these limitations is
put forth by the early Wittgenstein:

> . . . in order to be able to set a limit to thought, we should have to find
> both sides of the thinkable. *It will therefore only be in language that
> the limit can be set, and what lies on the other side of the limit will
> simply be nonsense.*[6]

This thinking on the other side of the limit is precisely what Lucky's
speech consists of. It is, however, not *non-sense*. Simple non-sense
would still be thought dictated by the dialectic of reason; it would
involve a simple crossing over to the other side of the dialectic –
doing or saying the *un*-reasonable thing – leaving its limits intact.
Lucky's think is not *unreasonable*; it is, to coin a word, *transreason-
able*: it does not simply offer us the other side of the dialectic of
reason, but moves at and beyond the margins of the dialectic, beyond
the limitations that have been placed on language. In Lucky's speech,
Beckett exposes and transgresses these limits, mixing bits of grammatical sense (inside the limit) and transgrammatical nonsense (outside
the limit) to the point where the limit itself is effaced, opening up the

field of what can be thought.[7] In Lucky's speech, Beckett attempts to show that – as Lyotard characterises the postmodern condition – 'there is no possibility that language games can be totalised in any metadiscourse' (p. 43). Through Lucky's speech, Beckett emphasises 'new "moves" and even new rules for language games' (p. 55), having transgressed and disrupted the old rules and limits.[8]

Lucky's think, though, meets with a less than enthusiastic response from the other characters on the stage. Vladimir, Estragon and Pozzo become increasingly uneasy during Lucky's tirade, until '*all three throw themselves on* **Lucky**, *who struggles and shouts his text*' (p. 28). Finally, after Lucky has been attacked and quieted, Pozzo grabs his hat (his 'thinking cap') and tramples on it, saying 'There's an end to his thinking!' (p. 30). This 'intellectual' violence, I think, mirrors the physical violence that Lucky is subjected to throughout the play.[9] According to the contemporary ethical thinker Emmanuel Levinas, there is a certain violence inherent in the make-up of objective metaphysical systems – as we have seen, they violently close off other possibilities, other forms of life.[10] Lucky's speech, then, can be seen as a peaceful one, transgressing the limits of an inherently violent coherence in objective metadiscourses. As Jacques Derrida writes in his essay on Levinas, 'Violence and Metaphysics':

> This coherence in ontology is violence itself for Levinas: the 'end' of history is not absolute Logic, the absolute coherence of the Logos with itself in itself, but peace in separation, the diaspora of absolutes. ... Is not peaceful discourse the discourse which respects separation and rejects the horizon of ontological coherence?[11]

Lucky's playful, 'peaceful' discourse is met with violence – intellectual and physical – because it disrupts the modernist notion of coherence in the grand Narrative: specifically, it disrupts the narrative upon which Vladimir and Estragon have based their existence, Godot. Lucky's speech is essentially peaceful because it displaces the notion of objective knowledge, a notion that moves hand-in-hand with power. Knowledge is power, and objectivist modern knowledge is always used to create or uphold a violent power structure. As Levinas writes, 'in history understood as the manifestation of reason, where *violence reveals itself to be reason*, philosophy presents itself as a realisation of being, that is, as *[philosophy's] liberation by the suppression of mutiplicity*. Knowledge would be the suppression of the other by grasp, by the hold, or by the vision that grasps before the grasp.'[12] Lucky's speech, though, points to a new, postmodern conception of knowledge. As Lyotard writes, 'postmodern knowledge is theorising its own evolution as discontinuous, catastrophic, non-rectifiable, and paradoxical. It is changing the meaning of the word *knowledge*. ... It is producing not the known, but the unknown' (p. 60).[13] Postmodern knowledge is not a tool for the bulwarking of the ruling power structure; rather, it moves at and beyond the limits of this structure – producing new ways to think about things, not simply data which reinforce and recuperate the old ways of thinking. Again, according to the ruling paradigm(s), much of this postmodern knowledge (Lucky's knowledge) may seem incomprehensible, but this is precisely the point because the postmodern drive is to push beyond the limits of the old paradigms. Vladimir and Estragon are at least on the right track when Vladimir says 'This is getting really insignificant', to which Estragon replies 'Not enough' (p. 44).

These lines, though, are not the only place in the play where we see Vladimir and Estragon on the verge of a Lucky-like postmodern breakthrough. In the course of the play it becomes increasingly apparent that Vladimir and Estragon are, relative to Godot, in the same servile position Lucky is, especially with respect to the doubly-violent end to his deconstructive think. For example, near the end of the play – after the boy has told Vladimir and Estragon that Godot again will not come today – we have this exchange:

Estragon	... Let's go far away from here.
Vladimir	We can't.
Estragon	Why not?
Vladimir	We have to come back to-morrow.
Estragon	What for?
Vladimir	To wait for Godot ...
Estragon	... And if we dropped him? (*Pause*) If we dropped him?
Vladimir	He'd punish us.

(p. 59)

Here we see Vladimir and Estragon on the verge of a deconstructive breakthrough, but again their dependence on the metadiscourse of Godot holds them back. In this passage, we see reiterated the violent nature of the limitations that a belief in Godot places on Vladimir and Estragon – both physical limits and, perhaps more importantly, intellectual ones: if they 'dropped him', they feel he would *punish* them. Vladimir and Estragon cannot leave the place they are in or think beyond the limits of a static, objective metasystem because of the rigid, violent limits placed on both their actions and their thought by the modernist metadiscourse represented by Godot. Their minds are slaves to Godot in the same way Lucky's body is a slave to Pozzo.

It seems to me that Beckett, throughout *Waiting for Godot*, is engaged in criticising the world view of the modernist, whose 'objective is to stabilise the referent, to arrange it according to a recognisable point of view which endows it with a recognisable meaning' (Lyotard, p. 74). I think Beckett refuses to allow his play (and the play of his play) to be put to such recuperative uses – although that is not to say that critics haven't tried. As a matter of fact, many interpreters allow for a cosy marriage between Beckett's drama and modernism, reading *Waiting for Godot* as, in essence, a lament for the lost grand Narrative – as revolving around a *lack* of meaning and possibilities. For example, Eugene Goodheart writes that in Beckett, 'the condition of nonbeing and meaninglessness is universal and insurmountable'.[14] This, it seems to me, is a *modern* reading of a *postmodern* writer.[15] Rather than revolving around a lack, *Godot*, as I read it, revolves around an *excess* of meaning and possibility brought about by the liberating notion of play. I do not see the play in Beckett as a 'kind of playing to *fill the void* of self',[16] but rather, as Derrida describes it, a postmodern play, a 'play whose other side would be the Nietzschean affirmation, that is the joyous affirmation of the play of the world and the innocence of becoming, the affirmation of a world of signs without fault, without truth and without origin which is offered to active interpretation. *This affirmation then determines noncentre otherwise than as loss of centre.* And it plays without security.'[17]

This *affirmation* of a noncentred world, this *rejection* of the grand Narratives, this *celebration* of play and language games is what most sharply separates the postmodern from the modern. In *Waiting for Godot*, Beckett shows us that Vladimir and Estragon are trapped by their modernist nostalgia for legitimation in Godot: they have a totalising, modernist world view in an infinite, postmodern world. From the beginning of the play, Beckett emphasises that this legitimation is always already there in the play of language games and the active interpretation of the postmodern, noncentred world – not in the passive, stifling waiting for the return of an objective grand Narrative that never really offered any metaphysical support in the first place. In the end, I think Beckett asks us to consider a world that, in Derrida's words, 'is no longer turned toward the origin, affirms play and tries to pass beyond man and humanism, the name of man being the name of that being who, throughout the entire history of metaphysics of ontotheology – in other words, throughout his entire history – has dreamed of full presence, the reassuring foundation, the origin and the end of play.'[18] In another of his dramas, *Endgame*, Beckett gives us a suitable epigraph for this – which I have argued to be *his* – postmodern world view:

> **Clov** (*imploringly*) Let's stop playing.
> **Hamm** Never![19]

From *Modern Drama*, 31 (1988), 520–8.

NOTES

[Jeffrey Nealon's essay belongs to a body of criticism that attempts to establish and explore the distinctiveness of 'postmodernist' culture. Among the claims for the postmodern made by such theories are that it breaks with the idealised or metaphysical certainties of previous eras, that it rejects the notion of the absolute distinctiveness and self-sufficiency of the artistic work, and that it favours relativity, complexity and incompleteness over every form of absolute, singular or total truth. Nealon draws on the work of Jean-François Lyotard to argue that *Waiting for Godot* is best apprehended as a transitional text, in which the characters are for the most part locked into a modernist desire for the ultimate legitimations of absolute truth and the metanarratives which guarantee them, but occasionally break through by a 'paralogy' or logically unpredictable move, into a postmodernist conception of social life as legitimated by the playing of a multiplicity of serious games. Ed.]

1. Ludwig Wittgenstein, *Philosophical Investigations*, trans. G. E. M. Anscombe (New York, 1958), sect. 23.

2. Frederic Jameson, 'Foreword', in Jean-François Lyotard, *The Postmodern Condition: A Report on Knowledge*, trans. Geoff Bennington and Brian Massumi (Minneapolis, 1984), p. xi. All further references to this text will be cited parenthetically.

3. Samuel Beckett, *Waiting for Godot* (New York, 1958), p. 10. All further references to this text will be cited parenthetically.

4. See pp, 10, 31, 44, 45, 54, and several other places in the text in a modified form.

5. Paul K. Feyerabend, *Against Method* (London, 1978), p. 27.

6. Ludwig Wittgenstein, *Tractatus Logico-Philosophicus* (Frankfurt, 1975), p. 7. Translated and cited in Allen Thiher's *Words in Reflection:*

Modern Language Theory and Postmodern Fiction (Chicago, 1984), p. 9.

7. Here I am making a perhaps problematical distinction between non-sense and nonsense. As I use the terms here, I mean sense to be taken as the reasonable end of the dialectic; non-sense is the other, unreasonable side. Nonsense lies outside the dialectic.

8. All of this is in opposition (non-dialectical I hope) to many readings of Beckett. For example, David Hesla argues that 'the shape of Beckett's art is the shape of the dialectic' (cited in Ann Paolucci's 'Pirandello and the Waiting Stage of the Absurd', *Modern Drama*, 23 [1980], 102–11, 109). My argument here is that Beckett's art moves not solely within dialectics, but at and beyond their margins.

9. In commenting on the play's physical violence in his essay 'Action and Play in Beckett's Theatre', *Modern Drama*, 9 (1966), 242–50, John Fletcher writes, 'In Beckett's drama, action is explored to the limit of the normally admissible and beyond' (243). Here I am arguing that in Beckett's drama *thought* is also explored to the normally admissible limit and beyond in Lucky's speech, triggering a reaction of 'intellectual' violence that mirrors the more obvious physical violence directed toward Lucky.

10. Levinas writes against thought 'fixed in the concept of totality, which dominates Western philosophy. Individuals are reduced to being bearers of forces that command them unbeknown to themselves. The meaning of individuals . . . is derived from the totality.' From his *Totality and Infinity*, trans. Alphonso Lingis (The Hague, 1969), pp. 21–2.

11. Jacques Derrida, 'Violence and Metaphysics', in *Writing and Difference*, trans. Alan Bass (Chicago, 1978), p. 315.

12. *Totality and Infinity*, p. 302, my emphasis.

13. Cf. Feyerabend's *Against Method*, pp. 17–28.

14. Eugene Goodheart, 'Literature as Game', *TriQuarterly*, 52 (1981), 134–49. For Goodheart, this meaninglessness is Beckett's 'discovery of the nature of things' (137).

15. As Lyotard writes, '[The] breaking up of the grand Narratives leads to what some authors analyse as the . . . disintegration of social aggregates into a mass of atoms thrown into the absurdity of Brownian motion. Nothing of this kind is happening: this point of view, it seems to me, is haunted by the paradisiac representation of a lost, "organic" society' (p. 15).

16. Goodheart, p. 137, my emphasis.

17. Jacques Derrida, 'Structure, Sign, and Play in the Discourse of the Human Sciences', *Writing and Difference*, p. 292.

18. Ibid., p. 292.

19. Samuel Beckett, *Endgame* (New York, 1958), p. 77. I must acknowledge that I have 'borrowed' the idea of using this quotation as an ending for my essay from John Fletcher's 'Action and Play in Beckett's Theatre' (cited above, n.9), although I use it in a different context to suggest a different network of ideas.

4

Counter-sensical Comedy and Audience Response in Beckett's 'Waiting for Godot'

WOLFGANG ISER

I

A basic feature of the technique in *Godot* is the unmistakable miscarriage of comedy. . . . The failed action, as one comic paradigm, . . . shows through action what is actually meant by 'nothing to be done'. Similarly, the repetition does not signify the futility of failed actions, but the fact that nothing can be learnt from failed actions. Consequently, the link between comic paradigms and overall plot is dislocated, so that the latter completely loses its syntagmatic function and the only relation left between the two different levels is one of mutual toppling. This instability results in a breakdown of the basic structure of comprehension, as syntagmatic and paradigmatic levels are flattened to equality and the interchangeability of their contents serves to emphasise the apparent futility of those contents. This levelling-out, however, produces a carnival effect, manifested in enjoyment of the nonsense, even though the tendency has disappeared upon which the inversions of the carnival or the relieving devices of comic pleasures are based.

It goes without saying that such dislocated comedy is bound to mobilise the interpretative faculties; indeed, if one might anticipate the effects produced by these structures, one might say that, in the manner in which the failure is presented, the artistry lies in the manipulation of these mobilised faculties. The comic paradigms, the mutally upsetting levels of action, the carnival effect, the enjoyment of nonsense, and finally the basic theme-and-background structure of perception and comprehension – all constitute 'minus functions', and this means that because of what they are, they always evoke that which they have excluded. Such a process continually compels the spectator to provide his own background, but at the same time it tells him nothing about why his expectations have been thwarted, or what sort of relationship exists between these thwarted expectations and what has actually been presented. He is therefore left with an array of empty spaces into which his mobilised interpretative faculties are relentlessly drawn and which are manipulated by them in a specific manner. For the purposes of laying bare the mechanics of this process, we will now try to give a schematised description of the interpretative activities triggered off by the play; we may thereby understand the text-guided processes occurring in the spectator's mind, and these in turn will serve as an indication of the kind of aesthetic experience which is to be imparted.

Vladimir and Estragon, the main characters, both seem to be tramps; we learn right at the beginning that Estragon spent the night in a ditch. But they also seem like clowns, as many critics have pointed out, although in fact neither 'tramp' nor 'clown' is ever mentioned in the text.[1] This clowning effect comes about through their constant failures and through their inability to learn from their failures, as evidenced by their endless repetitions. In Joachim Ritter's words: 'The clown is simply the outcast, the dropout, yet he proclaims this nonconformity not by the antithesis of meaning, but by an extreme distortion of it. His clothes are very different from normal clothes, but the long gloves, the countless jackets, the giant trousers represent a distortion, a perversion of ordinary dress. He carries around with him a meaningful piece of equipment, a garden-gate, but it is totally detached from its usual context, and so he uses it to keep entering the realm of nonsense, which becomes nonsense when set against sense, and thereby raises the liberating laughter that breaks down the barriers of seriousness and moderation.'[2] The laughter with which we greet the clown's actions is liberating because we perceive the naïveté in which he is trapped. Everything he does goes wrong, but he persists, as if the repetition denoted constant success. Such distortions are generally so absolute that the naïveté of the failure is immediately apparent, and so is greeted by immediate and spontaneous laughter. No mental activity is really required to put the distortion right, and the momentary perplexity can be relieved at once. The clown's naïveté places the spectator in a position of superiority which, as Freud observed, arises out of a comparison between the mental and spiritual qualities perceived in the comic character, and the qualities that determine one's own situation. The comparison of intellectual qualities is funny 'if the other person had made a greater expenditure than I thought I should need. In the case of a mental function, on the contrary, it becomes comic if the other person has spared himself expenditure which I regard as indispensable (for nonsense and stupidity are inefficiencies of function). In the former case I laugh because he has taken too much trouble, in the latter because he has taken too little.'[3] The clown's 'inefficiencies of function' signalise his being trapped in his naïveté, and it is precisely this impression that makes Vladimir and Estragon seem like clowns. People appear naïve if they do not know the restraints imposed by civilisation − restraints of which we ourselves are aware and which, in the given situation, we would also expect them to be aware of. We laugh at such people when, in their ignorance, they cross the borders of these restraints. In *Godot* these borders are set by the fact that the characters are waiting for Godot − a fact which seems to determine their whole lives, even though with their constant failures they behave as if the situation did not exist. Now if these characters seem to us like clowns, then we are already caught up in a process of interpretation; and in our efforts to find plausible reasons for the never ending repetition of failed actions, we ourselves become prisoners of the play.

Viewing the characters as clowns, or making them into clowns, is an interpretation arising out of a process of comparison which is comforting in so far as it enables one to reduce the unfamiliar to terms of the familiar, the abstract to the concrete, and so to master a strange and puzzling world. So long as Vladimir and Estragon represent comic paradigms through their repeated failures, we are misled into such a comparison. This is encouraged at first by the level of the overall comic plot-line. The characters are waiting for Godot; but they frequently behave as if they did not have any such purpose, and so we are constantly tempted to explain their conduct as naïveté; we begin to laugh because they constantly seem to transgress the limits set by their overall purpose. Our laughter is evidence of our position of superiority, but this position depends upon conditions that we have produced for ourselves. For this reason, our laughter does not make us happy; it has no cathartic effect because, at the very moment when we believe we can take the protagonists for clowns, this idea begins to fall apart owing to the increased indifference they show towards their avowed aim of waiting for Godot. Consequently our reaction is, in the last analysis, not to the clowning of the play, but to our own interpretation of it as clowning, which manifests itself in the flaring up and the dying down of our laughter.

This cut-off reaction is not due solely to the fact that we make the protagonists into clowns; it results in an even greater measure from a preconceived pattern of audience response that is built into the structure of the play. Whenever the diverse and apparently non-sensical actions seem to converge unequivocally into clowning, the characters suddenly relate once more, with detailed and often weighty allusions, to the overall plot-line of waiting for Godot. Biblical references to the crucified thieves,[4] an intricate casuistic debate, reminiscent of St Augustine, as to which of the thieves was saved,[5] Estragon's comparison of himself to Jesus,[6] all permeate the play with a density of allusions that have, logically enough, led many to conclude that the two men might in fact be waiting for God. But there is nothing in the text to confirm this, and Beckett himself, when asked who Godot was, merely replied that he would have said so if he had known it himself.[7] But whatever the heart of the matter may be, it is clear that our mobilised interpretative endeavours are guided in a certain direction. If these characters are waiting for God or some such all-powerful figure, if their identities are somehow connected with the thieves on the cross, then clearly we can no longer regard them as clowns. This means that we have erected a concept of the characters – admittedly with the guidance of the text – and are then forced to dismantle this concept as soon as we are made to relate the comic paradigms to the overall action.

Now in conventional comedy, the overall plot-line provides the background for the humour of the comic paradigms. In *Godot*, however, the overall plot-line seems to be the background against which the comic paradigms *lose* their humour. Naïveté as a source of comedy is not denied; but only when we ourselves deny its humour, does it become possible for us to relate the two levels of action to one another. And even if we were to persist in viewing the characters as naïve, this naïveté would be very dangerous in the light of their purpose, so that the situation would still take on a seriousness that would stifle our laughter. But whose is this seriousness? At times, it is true, the characters themselves cry out in despair, but we can never be sure of its extent or even its reality; at times we may project seriousness onto them without their knowing it; at times this projection of seriousness constitutes a perfectly natural and instinctive reaction akin to that of children at a pantomime, when they cry out to warn the unsuspecting hero that the villain is just behind him.

There is no need to go on illustrating these patterns of reaction, for one can already pinpoint the structure underlying and guiding the processing of such a text, as well as the function the structure is to perform. The play leads us into making a whole series of projections in order to provide some kind of overall background that will give coherence to the events we are witnessing. But, remarkably, our projections do not function as a substitute for cancelled expectations at all; on the contrary, we find ourselves compelled to abandon them. We conceive of the protagonists as clowns, but this view is upset by the allusions that deepen and intensify the dialogue. However, the apparent depth provided by the overall plot-line itself begins to topple when the characters fall back into the characteristic futility of their normal dialogue. The most striking features of this dialogue are its simplicity of syntax and vocabulary, the ease with which it can be understood, and above all the fact that it only describes what they do.[8] What is said means nothing but what in any case we can see – in other words, the language is purely denotative, so that we even begin to project intentions onto the absence of connotations. We feel ourselves being pushed into processes of interpretation because the actions denoted by the language seem to have no representative value, whereas the overall plot-line leads us to believe that there must be a representative value hidden somewhere. But if we think we have found such a value, it is quickly invalidated by the characters themselves. Furthermore we are tempted to project references onto the purely denotative language, but these are then wiped out whenever the dialogue itself becomes allusive. If we sense a pattern through the reference to the crucified thieves, it is wiped out by the fact that no one can say which of the thieves was saved, since even the apostles disagree.[9] What cannot be decided cannot be significant, and so the overall action ceases to impart any syntagmatic articulation to the comic paradigms; once the two levels come into contact, the overall plot-line is made trivial. The relation between the two levels is obviously such that whatever missing links the spectator may provide will at once begin to fall apart when they take on any degree of unequivocalness. Thus the view of the protagonists as clowns begins to topple when set against the Godot level; and the latter as a concept of possible salvation begins to topple when viewed against the protagonists' indifference.

This mutual destruction of interpretative concepts stimulated by the text does, however, constitute a 'connection' between the two levels of action, even if this connection is far from that which one would expect from a comic plot. Thus, the process of overturning our concepts – whatever their substance may be – implies that we are incessantly forced to build up a concept in the one instance, and then are forced to dismantle it in the next. It follows that the aesthetic object of the drama, which the spectator is always bound to assemble for himself in realising the intentions laid down for him, here comprises this very alternation of building and dismantling imaginary concepts. If one thinks back to the carnival effect, which permeates the whole atmosphere and construction of the play, the aesthetic object consists in the switching between what, for the sake of brevity, one might classify as clowning and salvation – two concepts which so undermine one another that they both disintegrate. Now with the carnival effect, as with one's enjoyment of nonsense, these confusing switches normally stabilise themselves by way of one tendency or another, but in Beckett's plays there is no tendency to latch onto, because the two levels of theme and background, or comic paradigm and overall plot-line, have been levelled out. But it is this very absence of any tendency that acts as a goad to the spectator's interpretative faculties, for an aesthetic object that constitutes itself through dismantling constructed concepts can only consolidate itself by means of a tendency. Any tendency in *Godot*, however, can only be in the form of a projection, as is only too clear from the well documented range of audience responses and interpretations since the play was first performed. Whatever the nature and substance of this projected tendency may be, it functions structurally as the syntagmatic articulation that balances out the 'minus function' of the overall plot-line of waiting for Godot, whose articulating force has become inoperative. It re-establishes the theme-and-background structure basic to comprehension, although it may remain completely open as to whether the comic paradigms are the background and waiting for Godot the theme, or vice versa. Our interpretation will vary according to which is which. When the prisoners of St Quentin recognised themselves in Vladimir and Estragon, the protagonists constituted the theme and the helpless waiting the background.[10] When the play is experienced as an existentialist apocalypse,[11] the helpless waiting is the theme, and the apathetic characters the background. In both interpretations one can see the compulsion to impose on the play a tendency which will allow a syntagmatic organisation of its paradigms.

Whatever the tendency projected onto the play, it is not an arbitrary act on the part of the spectator. It is the response to three central expectations relating to 1. the carnival effect and enjoyment of nonsense, 2. the theme-and-background structure of comprehension with its resultant organisation of the levels of action, and 3. the significance and precision necessary for each and every interpretation. Points 1 and 2 concern cancelled expectations pertaining to genre and cognition within the structure of the drama; point 3 denotes a basic requirement of comprehension in so far as meaning is only meaningful to the degree in which its significance is precise. As we have seen, the text of *Godot* undermines this basic requirement of meaning, and it is this process that gives rise to the peculiarity of the aesthetic experience offered by the play. For the continual building and dismantling of concepts that brings about the aesthetic object not only compels the projection of tendencies, but also challenges the significance essential to those tendencies. Thus the sense and the non-sense and the counter-sense of the play translate themselves into an experience for the spectator.

What *is* this counter-sense, and what are the reactions that such an experience can bring about? Counter-sense – as Plessner has emphasised[12] – is the basis of the comic situation. The counter-sense of *Godot* consists in the fact that on the one side we have the characters' incessant repetition of failed actions, and on the other the hopeless wait for an unforeseeable change through an unknown being. The spectator will react to these divergent themes by seeking a point of intersection. He can find one only to the extent that the protagonists' behaviour seems reduced to the level of clowning without actually *being* so, and the wait for salvation sinks into apathy without ever actually being lost from view. Thus the mutual distortion of the two 'senses' brings out a common element which we become aware of when we recognise that the source of these distortions is our own interpretations. In trying to impose significance and preciseness on the counter-sense, we experience our own interpretations as that which has been excluded by the counter-sense. Now this is also a comic effect, albeit an insidious one. If comedy focuses on that which is excluded by prevailing norms, thereby subverting their claim to comprehensiveness,[13] the resultant counter-sense will, in Beckett's case, keep drawing our interpretations into the play in order either to exclude them again on account of their incompleteness, or to unmask their distortive nature. In both cases, the projected norms of the spectator become part of the play, and there arises the effect which Beckett himself once described as his plays' 'clawing' into the spectator.[14] For the spectator is no longer confronted with a comic conflict; instead the comedy *happens* to him, because he experiences his own interpretations as that which is to be excluded. If the basic effect of comedy is to illuminate the whole of life[15] by showing the excluded striking back at the excluder (i.e. the norm), in Beckett this effect is inverted, as the spectator experiences the shortcomings of his interpretative norms just when he thinks they will enable him to grasp the whole.

This experience is conditioned by various factors connected with our own dispositions and, above all, with the expectations which we bring to art and which are deliberately exploited by Beckett's plays. The counter-sense in these plays does not come about by means of contrastive positions, such as one finds in traditional comedies. Instead it is present to us as an experience because, to begin with, we must formulate the aesthetic object by continually building and dismantling concepts, and ultimately – through this very same inescapable process – we are forced to realise (in both senses of the term) the incompleteness of our interpretations. However, the counter-sense of comedy has always been accompanied by a pattern which, so to speak, holds in store an overall resolution. It is the constant availability of such a pattern that allows us to remain detached from the events depicted and, furthermore, to experience these events as fiction rather than fact. So long as we live through the play as a presentation and not a reality, the events – particularly when the situation threatens danger – will always allow for a degree of distance, thereby providing the relief necessary to enable us to disentangle ourselves. But if the counter-sense is our very own experience, from which we cannot detach ourselves (because the attempt to free ourselves and to understand the experience reveals that even such attempts are only partial and restricted), then the situation seems to us more real than fictional. Here we have a comic structure which denies us the relief normally inherent in such structures. Freud once wrote: 'It is a necessary condition for generating the comic that we should be obliged, *simultaneously or in rapid succession*, to apply to one and the same act of ideation two different ideational methods, between which the "comparison" is then made and the comic difference emerges.'[16] But if this difference does not emerge, because the counter-sense is so total that any comparative operations will only succeed In uncovering their own inadequacies, then the comedy of the structurally comic situation will remain open-ended if not actually threatened with destruction. In conventional comedy, the differences resulting from the process of comparison point in the direction of a whole, albeit a whole that is signalised by way of transgressing limits that are caused by repression and by substitutions for taboos violated; but in Beckett's play the differences are wiped out by the continual overturning of the counter-senses, so that the whole can never be produced even though it is present in the toppling effect. This whole, evidenced only by the toppling effect of the counter-senses, might be described as the 'human condition', which can only be perceived as such by warding off every individual interpretation in order that it should not become a mere token for something other than itself. It cannot be referentially subsumed, and it cannot be represented either; it can only be experienced as a reality. And in experiencing this reality, we gain some insight into the very reality of this experience.

II

A presentation of the human condition through comedy seems in fact to be a logical continuation of the 'genre'; the play evokes specific expectations which it then proceeds to juggle with. The laughter which always greets the play might well be equated with the response expected in any comedy. But this laughter is of a very special kind. Joachim Ritter writes in his classic analysis of laughter: 'Laughter as a sound has its moment: namely, the precise moment at which comprehension has taken place, which is when the material has merged with the ideas already present in the listener or observer. However, this excludes the possibility that laughter should be attributed to particular layers of the inner being, particular moods, particular feelings during a particular "pleasure"; but at the same time it *in*cludes another implication: that laughter is only possible when an excluded and opposing idea can be grasped as an inalienable part of human existence; i.e. when it can be integrated as a meaningful component into this very existence.'[17] Now the laughter of Beckett's audiences does not seem to fit in with this definition at all. It has been noted time and again that the laughter that greets his plays is not contagious or communal. The latter category of mirth is confirmatory in its effect, for it communicates to others that 'an opposing idea' has been 'grasped as an inalienable part of human existence'.[18] But laughter at Beckett's plays is always isolated, apparently robbed of its contagious qualities; indeed in *Endgame* and *Happy Days* it is often accompanied by a sort of shock effect, as if the reaction were somehow inappropriate and must therefore be stifled.

The stifled burst of laughter is an individual reaction indicative of the breakdown of the liberating function of laughter. We normally laugh when our emotive or cognitive faculties have been overtaxed by a situation they can no longer cope with. 'The disorientated body takes over the response from it (i.e. the mind), no longer as an instrument for action, speech, movement or gesture, but simply as a body. Having lost control of it, having renounced any relation to it, man still evinces a sovereign understanding of the incomprehensible, displaying his power in his impotency, his freedom and greatness in his constraint. He can even find an answer where an answer is no longer possible. He has, if not the last word, at least the last card in a game whose loss is his victory.'[19] But in Beckett's theatre, this victory out of defeat turns into defeat again.

We have seen how, in Beckett's play, the different levels upset one another – an effect which becomes increasingly potent and virulent. The result of this mutual overturning is the collapse of the theme-and-background structure essential to comprehension. In attempting to stabilise this structure, we are forced to dismantle the tendencies we have projected onto the play. This means that the comic action, the structure of comprehension and the structure of participation all collapse the moment we try to stabilise them. This collapse involves the continual neutralisation of contrastive differences, and as has been shown by de Saussure and his structural semantics, if not by others before him, contrastive opposition is the basic condition of meaning. The toppling effect consequently cancels out each meaning as soon as it seeks to establish itself. This is the reason for the isolation of the laughers in Beckett's audiences. The timing of the toppling effect will largely depend on the disposition of the individual spectator, so that laughter as a reaction to and a relief from his entanglement is deprived of a collective confirmation at the very moment when it is most needed; the individual spectator then finds that he is laughing alone, and is thus made conscious of his own loss of control. This can be highly embarrassing. It should be borne in mind that inherent in the sound of laughter, in Plessner's words, 'is the power of self-affirmation: one hears oneself'.[20] But supposing one also sees oneself, because others are silent?

This brings us to the very special nature of the laugh that is elicited by the toppling effect. Freud made an interesting observation in his practice: 'Many of my neurotic patients who are under psychoanalytic treatment are regularly in the habit of confirming the fact by a laugh when I have succeeded in giving a faithful picture of their hidden unconscious to their conscious perception; and they laugh even when the content of what is unveiled would by no means justify this. This is subject, of course, to their having arrived close enough to the unconscious material to grasp it after the doctor has detected it and presented it to them.'[21] Now surprisingly, this observation coincides with a remark of Beckett's about laughter, which also sheds light on a strange feature of his plays: in *Godot*, *Endgame*, and *Happy Days* there are brief, violent bursts of laughter from the characters, that end as abruptly as they began. In Beckett's *Watt*, there is a short catalogue of laughs: 'Of all the laughs that strictly speaking are not laughs, but modes of ululation, only three I think need detain us, I mean the bitter, the hollow and the mirthless. They correspond to successive, how shall I say successive ... suc ... successive excoriations of the understanding, and the passage from the one to the other is the passage from the lesser to the greater, from the lower to the higher, from the outer to the inner, from the gross to the fine, from the matter to the form. The laugh that now is mirthless once was hollow, the laugh that once was hollow, once was bitter. And the laugh that once was bitter? ... The bitter laugh laughs at that which is not good, it is the ethical laugh. The hollow laugh laughs at that which is not true, it is the intellectual laugh. Not good! Not true! Well well. But the mirthless laugh is the dianoetic laugh ... It is the laugh of laughs, the *risus purus*, the laugh laughing at the laugh, the beholding, the saluting of the highest joke, in a word the laugh that laughs – silence please – at that which is unhappy.'[22] For Beckett, then, the real gradation of laughter begins where the laughter of comedy normally ends: with derision of that which is bad or malicious. But it is the mirthless 'laugh of laughs', the dianoetic mockery of unhappiness, that brings about its transparency and, interestingly enough, draws Freud and Beckett together. The raising of what has been displaced to the threshold of its perception allows one to face up to unhappiness, which in being faced is no longer exclusively itself, but appears in the perspective of its being perceived.

Unhappiness raised to consciousness is the source of dianoetic laughter. This observation would seem to explain the frequent, apparently unmotivated laughter of Beckett's characters. They burst out laughing when they have interpreted their own situations. Now if hollow and mirthless laughs are a response to untruth and unhappiness respectively, this means that the application of the cognitive faculties can no longer cope with that untruth and unhappiness. For such an intervention would inevitably lead to interpretations through which the unhappiness would not be raised but covered up and displaced even and so, in its ultimate effect, intensified because interpretations are commitments with a presumption of reality whereas when set against reality, their claims to authenticity fall apart. Laughter as a physical response to such a precarious situation is a last attempt at liberating oneself from a seemingly hopeless challenge; with our cognitive exertions stalled and our urge for interpretation (as a means of warding off unhappiness) frustrated, laughter remains as the one reaction that can cut itself off from unhappiness, thus banishing fear. It is true that Beckett's characters show, through their laughter, that they cannot avoid interpreting their situation; but at the same time they seem to know that clinging to such interpretations – even though these are doomed to eternal failure – embodies the source of untruth and unhappiness, the awareness of which announces itself through the physical reaction of laughter.

This laughter has no cathartic effect, but in its mirthlessness it is still a response to the human condition, which is lit up by the laughter and is accepted as itself and not as an interpretation of itself. If unhappiness arises from our need to stabilise our situation, our ultimate liberation would be to escape from the norms we have chosen or adopted in our efforts at stabilisation. And this is precisely what Beckett's characters are forever doing, which is why they seem so alien to us. This impression communicates itself through the extraordinary feeling that the characters, although they appear to behave like clowns, reveal a striking superiority which tends to efface the clowning element without removing it altogether. This is because they go the whole way in liberating themselves from the normally inescapable need to stabilise situations by means of interpretation, and their laughter marks the shattering of all self-imposed censorship. It has no healing power, for here the human condition presents itself, not as something that can be contained within prevailing systems of norms, but as something that demands continual explanations only in order to appear as itself by dissociating itself from these explanations. Such laughter is physical, and so elemental; it has no definable content of its own, because it lies beyond the scope of the defining intellect. In this respect, it is an entirely appropriate expression of the human condition, which is equally beyond definition and reveals itself only through an irremediable insufficiency of interpretative frameworks that are moulded, not by reality, but by man's need to explain reality.

The laughter and embarrassment with which Beckett's audiences react to a manifestation of the human condition indicates the fact not only that they are facing this condition, but also that they cannot cope with it. Why not? The answer can only be hypothetical, for as we have seen the laughter defies ultimate definition. It produces a mixed reaction in so far as it registers the nonsensical conduct of the characters who constantly turn aside from their own opinions and intentions; at the same time, however, we are unable to fulfil our enjoyment of the nonsensical by laughter, as we realise that the abandonment of purposes has a liberating effect on the characters. We see the tendency of the nonsense, but we do not understand it. Clearly, the laughter of the characters themselves destroys their own interpretations of precarious situations, for they seem to know that their unhappiness will only increase if they continue to seek compensatory resolutions. We, however, are not able to free ourselves in the same way, for we cannot suddenly regard our interpretations and guiding norms as nonsense. Consequently, we are left dangling, and our laughter dies. This position − being trapped halfway − is an almost insoluble paradox. Beckett's play compels us to construct the aesthetic object by continually building up and dismantling concepts, and through this process we are inescapably drawn into the experience that whatever objects we construct can only be a fashioning of objects − in other words, reality is never reality as such, but can only be a fashioning of reality. And yet we generally act as if our fashioning were identical to reality − i.e. as if our realities were more than mere fashioning. In fact they are simply pragmatic arrangements of reality, through which we gain security. Beckett's plays force us to develop a sense of discernment, so that we find ourselves playing off our need for security against our insight into the products of this need. Thus we come to the very borders of our own tolerance. But this is not the whole of the paradox. Beckett's play seems to dissatisfy us, because it makes us block our own paths to possible solutions. It is, however, not the play itself that denies us solutions;

we are 'left darkling' so long as we continue to identify with the world of our own concepts. This is a problem revealing and relevant for modern consciousness: we always long to be free from constraints, repressions and prefabricated solutions imposed upon us – and yet we are bewildered and shocked when such solutions are withheld from us in the theatre. Could it be that the ultimate source of laughter at Beckett's play is the fact that it confronts us with this unpalatable contradiction within ourselves? And could it be that this very same fact is also the source of irritation? If we were able to laugh in spite of it all, then laughter might – at least momentarily – indicate our readiness to accept our buried life, thus liberating it from the displacement caused by social and cultural repression. But are we really able to free ourselves from our unhappiness by facing up to it? Perhaps we might leave the final comment to Beckett himself, speaking through Nell in *Endgame*:

> **Nell** Nothing is funnier than unhappiness, I grant you that, But –
> **Nagg** (*shocked*). Oh!
> **Nell** Yes, yes, it's the most comical thing in the world. And we laugh, we laugh, with a will, in the beginning. But it's always the same thing. Yes, it's like the funny story we have heard too often, we still find it funny, but we don't laugh any more.[23]

From *Gestos*, 4 (1987), 21–32.

NOTES

[Wolfgang Iser has been one of the foremost and influential proponents of reader-centred literary theory over the last twenty years. His work has shown a close and continuous attention to the energetic interactions between text and reader required in particular by Beckett's work. The essay reprinted here is part of a longer study of the effects of 'stifled laughter' in Beckett's drama which appeared in German in 1979, and was reprinted by *Gestos*, a journal devoted to the theory and practice of Hispanic theatre published by the University of California at Irvine. In it, Iser focuses on the way in which *Waiting for Godot* forces its audience to become painfully conscious of the process of trying to make sense of the play, and in particular on the ambivalent laughter induced by the alternation between seriousness and nonsense in it. The references to the 'comic paradigms' of failed action and repetition in the first sentences of the essay refer to more detailed discussions in preceding sections which it has been necessary to omit for reasons of space. Ed.]

1. See Ruby Cohn, *Back to Beckett* (Princeton, 1973), p. 130; Ruby Cohn,

Samuel Beckett: The Comic Gamut (New Brunswick, 1962), p. 211; Beryl S. Fletcher, John Fletcher et al., *A Student's Guide to the Plays of Samuel Beckett* (London, 1978), pp. 38 and 45; Geneviève Serreau, 'Beckett's Clowns', in *Casebook on Waiting for Godot: The Impact of Beckett's Modern Classic: Reviews, Reflections and Interpretations*, ed. Ruby Cohn (New York, 1967), pp. 171–5.

2. Joachim Ritter, 'Über das Lachen', *Blätter für deutsche Philosophie*, 14 (1940/41), 14.

3. Sigmund Freud, *Jokes and Their Relation to the Unconscious*, Pelican Freud Library, vol. 6, trans. James Strachey (Harmondsworth, 1976), p. 255.

4. Samuel Beckett, *Waiting for Godot* (London, 1959), p. 12. All references are to this edition.

5. Ibid., pp. 12f.

6. Ibid., p. 52.

7. See Martin Esslin, *The Theatre of the Absurd* (New York, 1961), p. 12, where he quotes Beckett's reply to a question asked by the American director Alan Schneider.

8. For a more detailed discussion see my essay 'Samuel Beckett's Dramatic Language', *Modern Drama*, 9 (1966), 251–9.

9. *Waiting for Godot*, p. 13.

10. See Martin Esslin, '*Godot* at San Quentin', in Ruby Cohn (ed.), *Casebook on Waiting for Godot*, pp. 83–5.

11. See the material collected in *Casebook on Waiting for Godot*, as well as the following: Anon., 'They Also Serve', *TLS* (10 February 1956), p. 84 and readers' letters from J. M. S. Tompkins, *TLS* (24 February 1956), p. 117, Katherine M. Wilson, *TLS* (2 March 1956), p. 133, J. S. Walsh, *TLS* (9 March 1956), p. 149, Philip H. Bagby, *TLS* (23 March 1956), p. 181, William Empson, *TLS* (30 March 1956), p. 195, John J. O'Meara, *TLS* (6 April 1956), p. 207; and the leading article, *TLS* (13 April 1956), p. 221. See also Friedrich Hansen-Löve's essay 'Samuel Beckett oder die Einübung ins Nichts', *Hochland*, 50 (1957/8), 36ff. Günther Anders, *Die Antiquiertheit des Menschen* (Munich, 1956), p. 213, was one of the first to express basic doubts concerning any religious interpretation of this play shortly after its first publication.

12. Helmuth Plessner, *Lachen und Weinen: Eine Untersuchung nach den Grenzen menschlichen Verhaltens* (Bern, 1950), pp. 111f. and 121.

13. One of Ritter's fundamental definitions of comedy, in 'Über das Lachen', 9f.

14. See Hugh Kenner, *Samuel Beckett: A Critical Study* (New York, 1961), p. 165.

15. The degree to which the comic is always directed towards the totality of existence is dealt with more thoroughly by Ritter, 'Über das Lachen', 7 and 9.

16. Sigmund Freud, *Jokes and Their Relation to the Unconscious*, p. 300.

17. Ritter, 'Über das Lachen', 15.

18. Ibid.

19. Helmuth Plessner, *Lachen und Weinen*, p. 89.

20. Ibid., p. 90.

21. Sigmund Freud, *Jokes and Their Relation to the Unconscious*, p. 228 fn. 1.

22. Samuel Beckett, *Watt* (New York, 1959), p. 48. Regarding the conception of comic characters and the role as clowns in Beckett's novels, see Yasanuri Takahashi, 'Fool's Progress', in *Samuel Beckett: A Collection of Criticism*, ed. Ruby Cohn (New York, 1975), pp. 33–40.

23. Samuel Beckett, *Endgame* (New York, 1958), pp. 18f.

5

'Endgame': 'How Are Your Eyes?'

JANE ALISON HALE

Endgame, a one-act play for four characters, was written first in French and entitled *Fin de partie*. It premiered, in French, in April 1957 at London's Royal Court Theatre under the direction of Roger Blin.

The set of *Endgame* consists of a bare room bathed in grey light, with two small windows set high on the rear wall, one giving out onto the ocean and one onto land. There is a door to the right through which Clov, the servant, enters and leaves his kitchen; a picture hanging near the door with its face to the wall; two ashbins to the left which contain the legless couple, Nell and Nagg; and in the centre, an armchair on castors in which sits the blind and imperious Hamm – pitiless master of Clov, ungrateful son of Nell and Nagg, compulsive storyteller, and former tyrannical lord of an ill-defined, but now defunct, domain.

Hamm is blind; Clov manages, with some difficulty, to look out of the windows to report back to his master, and to the spectators, what he sees: Zero. Both men live in an enclosed shelter outside of which, in the words of Hamm, 'it's death'.[1] Both speak of leaving this space, Hamm through his death and Clov through abandonment of his master, yet the play leaves us with much doubt as to whether either will attain his goal.

Movement is a fundamental characteristic of the time and space of *Endgame*. Time passes; the characters 'get on'; yesterday and the future continually contaminate the present. Hamm, though confined

71

to his wheelchair, insists upon being wheeled around to the utmost limits of his room; Clov walks stiffly from window to window, in and out of his kitchen, and back to his master's side. Nell and Nagg, though maimed and confined to their ashbins, pop up and down so long as they are thought to be alive. There is indeed a great deal of movement in *Endgame*, yet nothing and nobody can actually be said ever to get anywhere, except perhaps a bit closer to an end whose very existence is uncertain.

The time and space of *Endgame*, as announced by its title, are those of an ending; the form and content of the play convey the impression of a world that is in gradual decline, where everything and everybody are weakening, winding down, running out. In spite of this progressive diminishment, however, the end toward which all seems to be moving is uncertain, unknown because unknowable, and perhaps unattainable. *Endgame* portrays a universe which is nearing its end but which seems likely to continue repeating itself, in an increasingly contracted form, forever. Beckett uses a variety of dramatic techniques to structure this picture of an ending, yet endless, time and space.

All of the characters suffer, to a greater or lesser degree, some physical deterioration: Hamm is blind and cannot use his legs; Clov sees, but his eyes are bad, walks, though with great difficulty, and cannot sit; Nell and Nagg have long ago lost their legs and Nell probably dies during the play. References are made to other people who once existed but have now died, some perhaps as a result of Hamm's abuse or neglect: Hamm's 'paupers', an old doctor, the navigators, Mother Pegg, a painter, a man who begged Hamm for food for his child one Christmas Eve. Life itself is defined in terms of degeneration: Hamm refutes Clov's assertion that 'there's no more nature' with the proof, 'But we breathe, we change! We lose our hair, our teeth! Our bloom! Our ideals!' and Clov is forced to admit, 'Then she hasn't forgotten us' (p. 11).

The décor of *Endgame* also contributes to the impression of a world coming to its end. Hamm refers to the room on stage as a 'shelter' (p. 3), and its bareness, grey light, and the grey nothingness of the barren, uninhabited world outside the windows all point to the distinct possibility that Hamm, Clov, Nell, and Nagg may be the last survivors of some dreadful catastrophe. (It is worth noting that, at the time Beckett wrote *Endgame*, the many hours spent in air-raid shelters during World War II were still vivid memories to most Europeans, and the horrors of impending nuclear war were becom-

ing a matter of widespread concern.) Even though a picture remains
on the wall of the room, it is turned over so its decorative function is
no longer served, and towards the end of the play Clov takes it down
to replace it with an alarm clock which, Hamm fears, is also nearing
its end. Hamm offers a possible clue to the origin of this enigmatic
picture when he tells Clov about a mad painter he once used to visit
in an asylum:

> I'd take him by the hand and drag him to the window. Look! There!
> All that rising corn! And there! Look! The sails of the herring fleet! All
> that loveliness!
> (*Pause.*)
> He'd snatch away his hand and go back into his corner. Appalled. All
> he had seen was ashes.
>
> (p. 44)

The situation Hamm describes contains some striking parallels with
his own present existence in the shelter with Clov, who also takes his
companion to the windows of the room and describes what he sees
on the earth and in the sea. Hamm's correction of the tenses he uses
in summing up his narration of these visits suggests the extent to
which he identifies with the mad artist: 'It appears the case is . . . was
not so . . . so unusual' (p. 44). However, where Hamm had described
a landscape of colour and beauty to his friend, who could perceive
nothing but the undifferentiated greyness of ashes, Clov and Hamm
have each moved one step further away from traditional vision in
perspective: Hamm is totally blind, and the person who serves as his
visual interpreter of the world reports that earth and sea have turned
grey. Visions like the one Hamm describes here from memory are
mentioned throughout *Endgame*, and they always belong either to a
distant past, like this one and like the old folks' memory of their
romantic boat ride on Lake Como, or to a dream, as when Hamm
speaks of going into the woods in his sleep, where 'My eyes would
see . . . the sky, the earth . . . Nature!' (p. 18). If such visions were
once possible, they are clearly so no longer. It is thus fitting that the
painting should be turned to the wall, and finally removed, in a
universe where coloured landscapes seen through the imaginary
window of a painting in perspective have turned to a flat, barren,
uncertain greyness that offers only fleeting, fragmentary, indistinct
images to the eye of the observer. Clov's replacing of the picture with
an alarm clock late in the play underscores the relationship between
painting and time: the mobile, endless, aimless, repetitious time of

Endgame's universe renders obsolete a form of art that grew out of a different conception of time (and space).

If the characters' physical appearance and the décor of *Endgame* convey the visual impression of an ending, its text fills our ears with references to the end. From the very first line of the play, when Clov announces, 'Finished, it's finished, nearly finished, it must be nearly finished' (p. 1), we hear allusion after allusion to the end of time, of people, of stories, of food, of objects, of nature, of colour, of sight, of fleas and rats, of light, of the day, of love, of the meaning of words, of the earth and sea, of laughter, of weather, of the sun, of kisses, of clocks, of spring, of God, of sound, of motion, of song, of beauty, of order, of the game played by Hamm and Clov, of all 'This . . . this . . . thing' (p. 45). Just as time is running out, so are all the people, attributes, and objects that once composed the universe. Clov and Hamm engage over and over again in a comically repetitive exchange where Hamm asks Clov to observe or give him something, and Clov responds, 'There are no more'. Over the course of the play, there are, successively, 'no more': bicycle-wheels, pap, nature, sugar-plums, tides, navigators, rugs, pain-killer, and coffins.

This diminution of the elements of the universe, as well as the impression conveyed that the world surrounding Hamm's and Clov's shelter is in ruins, suggest a possible interpretation of *Endgame* as a perverted parody of the Noah's ark myth.[2] While in Genesis the Lord commanded Noah, father of Ham, to build an ark with a window and a door and to furnish it with representatives of all living species in order to insure the continuance of his creation after the great flood, Beckett's Hamm makes every effort to see that his refuge, which, like Noah's ark, contains the last supply of food in the world, will engender no further life, not even so much as a future generation of fleas or rats. The many references to animals in *Endgame* add credence to the Noah's ark analogy. The names of the characters all suggest various animals: Hamm, the flesh of the pig; Clov, the spice used to cure ham; Nell, a common name for a horse; and Nagg, a word used to describe an old, worn-out horse.[3] At one point, Nagg sucks on a dog biscuit called 'Spratt's medium' (p. 10), and Clov later presents Hamm with a toy dog he has been making for his master. The nobility of Noah's mission to save human and animal life is savagely parodied in Beckett's version of the story, where the animals chosen to inhabit the refuge represent the lowest, dirtiest, most useless, annoying, or comical forms of life: a rat, a flea, and an artificial dog with three legs and no sex. The people are likewise far removed from the righteousness and fertility of Noah's family. Physically and spiritually sterile, they present a bleak outlook for the future of humanity. The death of Nell, the last female of the group, seems to confirm the impossibility of the reproduction of the species, although even in life she had for some time been unable to have any form of physical contact with her husband.

Charles Lyons sees in *Endgame* an ironic reversal of another biblical account, that of the creation of the world. In his provocative essay, 'Beckett's *Endgame*: An Anti-Myth of Creation',[4] he presents a fascinating and coherent reading of the play as a depiction of the disintegration of the universe as perceived by a dying consciousness. While God created the world by separating the earth from the waters and by creating light, Beckett shows us a universe where the earth and waters, as perceived by Clov from the two windows of the set, come to resemble each other more and more, as they are reduced to 'grey' and 'zero', and where people like Mother Pegg die for lack of light.

Even though time, space and life are winding down in *Endgame*, they are not certain ever to die out altogether. Just when Hamm, Clov and the audience are convinced that outside the room shown on stage all is indeed zero, grey and death, Clov reports the sighting of a small boy whom he identifies as a 'potential procreator' (p. 78). Clov has gone to great pains during the play attempting to destroy a rat he found in his kitchen and to kill a flea which invaded his pants, in order to please Hamm, who fears that 'humanity might start from there all over again!' (p. 33). It therefore comes as somewhat of a surprise to him, and to us, when Hamm forbids Clov to go after the boy with a gaff, explaining, 'If he exists he'll die there or he'll come here. And if he doesn't . . .' (p. 78). Whether he dies there, comes into the shelter (perhaps to replace Clov if he leaves or Hamm if he dies), or doesn't exist, the regenerative potential suggested by this boy calls the possibility of there being an end to 'this . . . thing' (p. 45) into question. The original French play devotes many more lines than the English to this episode and describes the boy in greater detail: immobile, seated on the ground leaning against a rock, he contemplates his navel. The French text also shows a change in Hamm's attitude, from an initial desire to exterminate the boy to a philosophical resignation to his possible existence. In addition, it alludes both to the stone that was rolled away from Christ's tomb and to Moses' dying vision of the promised land. Martin Esslin has suggested that, when Clov contradicts Hamm's comparison of the boy to the dying Moses, but not the image of the lifted stone connected with the resurrection, he reinforces the idea of birth and reproduction suggested by the boy's fetal position.[5] In both versions, the incident with the little boy strongly suggests that the outside world may not be as dead as we might have believed, and that the ending so long awaited with both fear and eagerness by Hamm and Clov may be yet a while, perhaps forever, in coming.

Another aspect of *Endgame* that serves to cast doubt upon the possibility of any ending to the game being played out before our eyes is Hamm's persistent effort at storytelling, and especially his seemingly futile desire to bring his story to a close. The tale he relates to his captive audience – his parents, his servant, and the spectators in the theatre – may well be autobiographical. We know that Hamm, like the rich gentleman in his first-person narrative, was once the master of a large domain who took pleasure in refusing aid to the less fortunate creatures that depended upon him. The child whom his character was asked to take in against his wishes may well be Clov, and the ending to his story that keeps eluding him may coincide with the equally elusive ending of his own life. Clov makes evident the coincidence between Hamm's story and his life in the following exchange: '**Hamm**   What story? **Clov**   The one you've been telling yourself all your days' (p. 58). Hamm describes the progress he is making on his story in the same terms he uses to evaluate his life with Clov and his parents: 'I've got on with it' (p. 59). Though Hamm feels compelled to continue his chronicle, he fears its end, but Clov reassures him that, should the conclusion be reached, 'You'll make up another' (p. 61). Hamm would prefer to put a definitive end to 'the prolonged creative effort' that has been draining him, to drag himself down to the sea where 'I'd make a pillow of sand for my head and the tide would come' (p. 61), for the only way he can imagine an end to his storytelling is to imagine an end to his life. However, even though the idea of ending has obsessed Hamm throughout his existence, just as it has been a constant theme and image of *Endgame* from the first moment of the play, the end may never be reached. As Hamm concludes, in an ironic recasting of a biblical verse, 'The end is in the beginning and yet you go on' (p. 69).

When Hamm speaks of ending his tale, he foresees, like Clov, that another will come to take its place: 'Perhaps I could go on with my story, end it and begin another' (p. 69). He dreams of 'the end', which has been 'so long coming', when he will be 'in the old shelter, alone against the silence and . . . the stillness', where, 'if I can hold my peace, and sit quiet, it will all be over with sound, and motion, all over and done with' (p. 69). The 'if' is of cardinal importance here, for it postulates a state of immobility as the precondition for the end. Since immobility is impossible in the Beckettian scheme of existence, so, it would seem, is the end. Hamm's words recall an earlier statement made by Clov to explain why he was straightening up the objects in the room on stage: 'I love order. It's my dream. A world where all would be silent and still and each thing in its place, under the last dust.' Here again, stillness is the prerequisite for the end, and it is once more impossible, a mere dream. Realising this, Clov does not object when Hamm orders him to drop the things he has picked up, and he remarks with resignation, 'After all, there or elsewhere' (p. 57). For in the world in which he lives, each thing does not have its place, since order, silence and stillness are impossible, and the last dust may therefore never come to fulfil his dream. Hamm, too, acknowledges the futility of his desire for the stillness which would allow 'it [to] . . . be all over and done with'. As he serenely envisions his solitude in the old shelter where he would wait for his end, he suddenly becomes agitated when he realises that the peace he longs for will be withheld even there. For, though he may succeed in withdrawing from the world outside his shelter, and in driving away the last companions he has within it, he will be unable to put an end to the process of self-perception, which he describes as 'All kinds of fantasies! That I'm being watched! A rat! Steps! . . . Then babble, babble, words, like the solitary child who turns himself into children, two, three, so as to be together, and whisper together, in the dark' (p. 70). It is indeed entirely possible that this is the situation in which we now see Hamm: alone at last in the old shelter, he may be merely imagining the watchful presence of Clov, Nell and Nagg, splitting himself into the various characters of *Endgame* in order to maintain the condition necessary for the continuation of the human conscious-ness – the subject/object dichotomy.

Hamm comments upon his story's progress with the same self-consciousness he displays when he critiques the game in which he and Clov are engaged; his life in the shelter is in many respects a living proof that 'all the world's a stage'. His name recalls both the main character of *Hamlet*, Shakespeare's greatest 'play-within-a-play', and his role as a 'ham actor' in the drama of human existence. Hamm's 'chronicle' is a story-within-a-story-within-a-story, in a seemingly endless procession of characters and dialogue. His rela-tionship and verbal exchanges with Clov are no less contrived and self-consciously dramatic than the story he 'makes up'. Indeed, all the characters of *Endgame* reflect upon their speech and actions using the vocabulary and cynical objectivity of experienced drama critics: 'We're getting on' (p. 9); 'This is slow work' (p. 12); 'Why this farce, day after day?' (p. 14); 'What does that mean?' (p. 20); 'Will this never finish?' (p. 23); 'This is deadly' (p. 28); 'Things are livening up' (p. 29); 'I see ... a multitude [the audience] ... in transports ... of joy' (p. 29); 'What's happening?' (p. 32); 'Do you not think this has gone on long enough?' (p. 45); 'Got him that time!' (p. 49); 'Our revels now are ended' (p. 56 – cf. Shakespeare's *The Tempest*, IV.i); 'What is there to keep me here? ... The dialogue' (p. 58); 'Ah let's get it over!' (p. 70); 'I'm tired of our goings on' (p. 76); 'Let's stop playing!' (p. 77); 'Let it end!' (p. 77); 'An aside, ape! Did you never hear an aside before? ... I'm warming up for my last soliloquy' (pp. 77–8); 'Not an underplot, I trust' (p. 78); 'Articulate!' (p. 80); 'This is what we call making an exit' (p. 81); 'Nicely put, that' (p. 83); 'Since that's the way we're playing it ... let's play it that way' (p. 84).

The technique of presenting a play-within-a-play, or a story-within-a-play-within-a-play, gives the spectator an impression of being led into a hall of mirrors, where images and situations lose their identity and precise contours as they are reflected in an endless labyrinth of change and flux. We have no way of knowing for certain where Hamm's story ends and the saga of Hamm and Clov begins, or if Hamm and Clov might suddenly decide to bring the game they are playing to an end only to recommence another in this, or a different, place with these, or other, characters.

The cessation of the consciousness, the end of existence, immobility and silence – all are merely impossible dreams for Hamm. The only solution to the endless game of perception in which he feels trapped is equally impossible: 'Breath held and then ... ' (p. 70). Hamm seems to be speaking here of suicide by apnoea, which Beckett described in the following manner in *Murphy*: 'Suicide by apnoea has often been tried, notably by the condemned to death. In vain. It is a physiological impossibility' (p. 185). Earlier in the same novel, birth is defined as 'the moment of ... being strangled into a state of respiration' (p. 71). Thus, existence, which is characterised by breathing and which is savagely forced upon our unwilling bodies at the beginning, is equally implacable at the end: our breath will not stop, no matter how much we might will it to do so, and the end so longed for by Hamm continues to elude him. Hamm sums up his reflections on the problem of not being able to end either his story or his life with a poignant reference to one of Zeno's paradoxes: 'Moment upon moment, pattering down, like the millet grains of . . . that old Greek, and all life long you wait for that to mount up to a life' (p. 70). These words echo Clov's from the beginning of the play: 'Grain upon grain, one by one, and one day, suddenly, there's a heap, a little heap, the impossible heap' (p. 1). The moments of existence, which can never add up to make a life because they are endless and in constant motion, are like the pile of millet grains which Zeno proposed splitting in half, then in half again, and again, and again, ad infinitum, in a process that could come to an end only in a time and space unknown to, and unperceivable by, the human consciousness. It is characteristic of Beckett's fine sense of irony that he chose a paradox created by a philosopher whose goal was to prove the impossibility of movement in order to illustrate his own conception of the impossibility of immobility.

Describing time in terms of grains 'pattering down' into a heap also brings to mind a common image of time: that of an hourglass filled with grains of sand. Although the flow of sand in an hourglass does come to an end, the process can be renewed continuously by turning over the glass to set the grains in motion again. In much the same way, the action, time, space, and speech of *Endgame* come to rest after Hamm's final soliloquy, yet we know that all will recommence when the play is repeated for a subsequent audience. The silent tableau at the end of the play may thus be nothing more than the moment Hamm describes when he says 'Breath held and then . . .'; the 'fantasies' of perception, animals, motion, babbling voices, and moment piling upon moment as he waits to 'get it over' which are the substance of *Endgame* are likely to flow on forever, subject to brief pauses, and slight changes in their order of occurrence, just like the sands of time in an hourglass.

If Hamm's inability to finish his story, or his life, underscores the endless nature of Beckettian time, the question of Clov's departure, a constant theme from the beginning of the play, presents a similar conception of space. He clearly desires to leave and often announces his intention to do so to Hamm; at the end of the play he appears dressed for travel and remains impassive and motionless as Hamm delivers his final speech. We will never know for certain if he succeeds in leaving, since he is still standing at the door when the curtain falls. Clov's very name underlines the ambiguity of his situation, since *clove* is the past participle of the verb *to cleave*, a word which means, oddly enough, both *to separate* and *to adhere*. Clov's position at the end of the play recalls that of Didi and Gogo at the end of *Waiting for Godot*, when the exchange, '**Vladimir** Well? Shall we go? **Estragon** Yes, let's go', is followed by the indication, '*They do not move. Curtain*' (p. 60). In both cases, Beckett creates doubts in our minds as to the future actions of his characters by juxtaposing contradictory dialogue and stage directions. We cannot be sure if Clov will leave, but we do know that he hasn't done it yet, and we have had several indications over the course of the play that such a departure would be impossible, e.g. '**Hamm** You can't leave us. **Clov** Then I won't leave you' (p. 37). In two separate passages, Clov sums up his predicament and makes clear the reason he will never be able to leave: 'There's nowhere else' (p. 6); 'I say to myself – sometimes, Clov, you must be there better than that if you want them to let you go – one day. But I feel too old, and too far, to form new habits. Good, it'll never end, I'll never go' (p. 81). What prevents Clov from going is the indeterminacy of space: there is nowhere else than the endless, formless, inescapable space he has always inhabited because a 'there' can exist only by contrast with a well-defined 'here'; he would have to 'be there', i.e. experience a sense of place, better than he knows how, in order to be able to conceive of a different space to which he might escape. Hamm had earlier expressed the same idea when he announced to Clov, 'Do you know what it is? . . . I was never there . . . Absent, always' (p. 74). For both the characters in the play and its spectators, the only time and space of *Endgame*'s universe exist on the stage; outside all is grey, zero and death. Just after Hamm tells Clov that he 'was never there', he poses a question which many spectators of *Endgame* must have asked their fellow theatregoers: 'Do you know what's happened?' Clov's response takes the form of two essential questions: 'When? Where?' (p. 75). In order for a definable 'something' to happen, it must occur in an identifiable, discrete, time and place. When any one of these elements breaks down, so must the others, and their dissolution puts an end to the linear perspective of post-Renaissance drama, with its well-made plots and unities of time (when?), place (where?), and action (what's happened?). Beckett's response to the question of 'what happens' in *Endgame* is adamant in its refusal to define the undefinable: 'Hamm as stated, and Clov as stated, together as stated, nec tecum nec sine te, in such a place, and in such a world, that's all I can manage, more than I could.'[6]

At one point in *Endgame*, Hamm announces to Clov, 'Gone from me you'd be dead' (p. 70). It does indeed seem that though Clov cannot stand to live with his difficult master, he would not be able to exist without him. This *'nec tecum nec sine te'* relationship, which is similar to that of Didi and Gogo in *Waiting for Godot*, has been used, like the one between the two tramps, to support a reading of *Endgame* as a representation of a human consciousness.[7] The scene may be taken to suggest the interior of a human skull, a privileged image for Beckett, especially in his novels. The two windows would be the eyes; the grey light would evoke the grey matter of the brain. The four characters might represent diverse elements of a single human personality: Hamm would be the inner 'me', irrational and emotional (this would explain his sudden, savage mood changes); Clov would be the rational 'me' who maintains contact with the external world; Nell and Nagg could be simply memories that are weakening and disappearing – the act of putting the lids on the ashbins would thus represent an attempt to repress painful memories. Hamm and Clov live in a symbiotic state; the blind Hamm depends upon Clov's sight, and since he is paralysed, he could not survive were Clov not there to feed him; since Clov does not know the combination of the cupboard where the food is kept, he would die of hunger without his master. According to this interpretation, *Endgame* would thus present an image of the dissociation of a human consciousness in the last minutes before death: the death of the exterior world resembles the dissolution of ties with outer reality that occurs in a dying mind. The final stalemate of this endgame portrays the paradox of human consciousness which is omnipresent in Beckett's work: the consciousness can never attain a definitive end, because it would be unable to perceive the nothingness that it would meet there. At the end of *Endgame*, or of his life, Hamm will not know for certain if Clov has left, for if Clov leaves, Hamm will die and thus be incapable of perceiving Clov's absence.

Beckett leads the spectators to understand Hamm's perceptual dilemma by producing similar uncertainties in our minds regarding both Clov's departure and Hamm's death. When the final curtain is drawn, Clov is preparing to go, and Hamm has delivered his 'last soliloquy' (p. 78), called his father and his servant, with no response, and covered his face with his handkerchief. It would indeed seem that Hamm has finally been able to reach his end, yet when we remember the beginning of the play, the ending seems less certain. Just as Clov opened *Endgame* with the word 'finished', Hamm has closed by repeating one of his first lines – 'Old stancher!' – and by replacing the handkerchief that he had removed from his face at the beginning of the play. It is entirely possible that Clov will proceed to cover the ashbins and Hamm with sheets and then retire to his kitchen while Hamm sleeps, only to return to his master's side the following morning when he will remove the sheets, announce once more that 'it's finished, nearly finished', and recommence his game with Hamm. Once again, the existence we are witnessing upon the stage finds a parallel in the nature of the theatre: *Endgame* will indeed begin again tomorrow, before a different audience, with slight variations in its performance and reception, taking as its point of departure the announcement of its ending. We thus become aware of yet another level in the series of plays-within-plays in which we have become embroiled: from Hamm's chronicle to his self-conscious ham acting for his family and for the larger audience in the theatre, we are led to consider the single performance of *Endgame* that we have viewed as merely one repetition in a potentially infinite series of productions which begin at the end, and end at the beginning, and yet go on. Beckett has succeeded in creating a dramatic form for *Endgame* that corresponds to our contemporary notions of time and space. More traditional forms of drama, which present linear plot developments with clear-cut beginnings, climaxes, and conclusions, were appropriate for audiences who believed that human life and history were organised in the same manner. At one point in the play, Clov attempts to bring the action to a close by borrowing one of the traditional forms of a theatrical finale: song (p. 72). Hamm stops him with the command, 'Don't sing', and when Clov inquires, 'One hasn't the right to sing any more?', Hamm's response is 'No'. Clov's next question, 'Then how can it end?', goes unanswered, for the days when lives and plays could end may be gone forever. Thus, the most optimistic reply we can offer to Hamm's exasperated and furious question, 'Will this never finish?' (p. 23), is Clov's unconvincing 'It may end' (p. 5).

If *Endgame* may end, it may not, either. Hamm may be a king in stalemate position when the curtain closes, not yet in check, but unable to move into any other position, approaching his end, yet never attaining it. Many critics have pointed out the relationships between *Endgame* and the game of chess, which inspired its title. Hamm's first words, 'Me . . . to play' (p. 2), are repeated in his final speech, after which he refers to the 'old endgame lost of old' (p. 82), and says, 'Since that's the way we're playing it . . . let's play it that way' (p. 84). Like the game of chess, *Endgame* is rigidly structured and both the game and the play take the form of a progressive stripping away of elements from an enclosed space. Like pieces on a chessboard, the characters of *Endgame* are severely restricted in their movements, each obeying a different rule of motion (e.g. Hamm can sit but cannot stand, while Clov can stand but cannot sit). The frequent 'pause', which is by far the most common stage direction in *Endgame*, helps to structure the play like a chess game where each player reflects silently before proceeding with his next move. Beckett's affinity for the game of chess is a well-known fact, perhaps most evident in his novel *Murphy*, but present throughout his work. The colours of chess, white and black, have become the predominant colours of his latest works, and he has long been fascinated with experiments in permutation, the fundamental principle of the game of chess.

In *Homo ludens*, a study of the social function of games and play, J. Huizinga defines the characteristics of games in terms that help us to understand the motivation underlying all the games played by the characters of *Endgame*. A game, he says, is played to create order, to lend a temporary, limited perfection to a confused and imperfect world. It takes place in an expressly circumscribed, clearly limited time and place, beginning at a given moment and continuing until its end, which is easily recognisable. It follows a specific and absolute order created by an arbitrary set of rules that are freely consented to by all players. Situated outside the sphere of utility and material necessity, it is experienced as 'fictitious' by the participants, who nevertheless become completely absorbed by it. A game is conducted in an atmosphere of enthusiasm, accompanied by the tension created by elements of uncertainty and chance, and its end is characterised by feelings of joy, relaxation, and release.[8] It is no wonder, then, that Hamm and Clov seize upon every possible opportunity to play games in a universe that is without order, imperfect, and in which time and space are unlimited, undefinable and unperceivable.

B. S. Hammond has pointed out the importance of the game theme in *Endgame* as a means of imposing structure upon a world which has none:

> In a world no longer rendered purposeful by Christian conceptions of eschatology, time is experienced not as a linear development towards a goal, but as a yawning vacuum, a black hole without structure. Structure has to be imposed from without through routine and, for Beckett's characters, through the playing of games. The games Hamm and Clov play are futile, but they are all there is.[9]

Beckett's choice of a chessboard to structure *Endgame*'s universe brings to mind another instance in which chessboards were used to structure art: painting in linear perspective. Time and time again in these paintings a floor is laid out in a chequered pattern whose receding lines organise the entire picture space. Beckett borrows this longstanding aesthetic tradition and adapts it to his new dramatic perspective; his characters attempt to play out their lives according to rules formulated in and for another era, and they seem doomed to an endless, repetitious, meaningless series of movements in a space that is no longer rational, measurable and comprehensible like the one of the paintings whose chequered floors led the observer's eye to their central vanishing point. Instead of succeeding in bringing their game to an orderly end, they move blindly and confusedly on a chessboard that seems to exist only as a nostalgic relic of an era when vision was possible.

Beckitt employs several other traditional images of vision and perspective in similar fashion – the objects remain although they no longer fulfil their former functions. Eyes, for example, are prevalent in *Endgame*. Hamm's blind eyes have 'gone all white' (p. 4), and he can see only through the eyes of Clov, which are 'bad' (p. 7), and which, he prophesies, will continue to get worse until 'one day you'll be blind, like me. ... Infinite emptiness will be all around you' (p. 36). Although Hamm wears glasses and Clov uses a telescope to assist his exploration of the world beyond the window, these optical aids seem to have outlived their usefulness and exist only as vestiges of an earlier time when people believed in the possibility of perfecting vision by using instruments of their own invention.[10] Likewise, the set of *Endgame* contains two windows, the conventional frame through which spectators view a scene in perspective, yet the windows no longer function as before – they offer a vista which Clov sums up as 'Corpsed', 'All gone', 'Lead', 'Zero' and 'Gray' (pp. 30–1). The picture hanging beside the windows is similarly obsolete – it is merely a reminder of the bygone days when one could see, and paint, fields of corn and fleets of ships, when nature was visible and comprehensible to human eyes.

Hamm has retreated to an enclosed shelter, perhaps in an effort to define a space for himself that would permit vision by affording a definable and stable point of view upon the world around him: he insists upon Clov's wheeling him around to the limits of his room, then back to its exact centre, so that he can perceive and comprehend the space in which he exists. Yet the effort is futile, for the walls are boundaries between Hamm's universe and the nothingness that lies beyond, merely 'hollow bricks' dividing this place from 'the . . . other hell' (p. 26). Since there is nothing on the other side, they are unattainable, in spite of Hamm's violent urgings to 'hug the walls' and go 'Closer! Closer! Up against!' (pp. 25–6). His desire to be replaced in the exact centre of the room is just as vain, since a centre can be defined only in relation to precise boundaries, and boundaries can exist only if they delimit one space from another. So Hamm's attempt to separate his own space from the one he wishes to observe is a failure, since the only space available for observation is that in which he exists. In spite of his glasses, the windows of his room, and all his efforts to perceive the ends of the time and space of his life, he can put nothing in perspective, since he can attain no stable, exterior, definable point of observation, and admits to having lost the game he has been playing: 'Old endgame lost of old, play and lose and have done with losing' (p. 82). He realises that his story, like the play in which he stars, will end in darkness, with no conclusion: 'Moments for nothing, now as always, time was never and time is over, reckoning closed and story ended' (p. 83).

From Jane Alison Hale, *The Broken Window: Beckett's Dramatic Perspective* (West Purdue, 1987), pp. 45–60.

NOTES

[The book from which Jane Alison Hale's essay is taken focuses upon Beckett's treatment of perception, space and time, arguing that his work undermines that structure of perspective which has dominated Western culture since the Renaissance, a structure which depends upon the orderly and stable disposition of the viewing subject in relation to the spaces and objects that it views. This structure in turn seems to guarantee the comprehensibility of time and the individual self's capacity to know itself. Beckett's work, in common with that of many artists and writers in the twentieth century, enacts and represents much more complex and unstable models of time and space. *Endgame* in particular, she argues, seems to show characters who are vainly trying to hold on to ideas of stable, knowable space and coherently progressive time, in a world in which neither of these can be relied upon. The particular mark of this failure is the deterioration of vision, which no longer seems to guarantee the stability of perspective or the possibility of clear perception. In undermining our own sense of coherent space as viewers in the theatre, Beckett makes this disorientation actual as well as theoretical. Ed.]

1. Samuel Beckett, *Endgame, followed by Act Without Words* (New York, 1958), p. 9. All references will be to this edition and incorporated parenthetically in the text.

2. See Ruby Cohn, *Samuel Beckett: The Comic Gamut* (New Brunswick, 1962), pp. 226–42, for a discussion of this as well as numerous other biblical references in *Endgame*.

3. Ibid., pp. 229, 233, 236 and 241, for this and further interpretations of the names of *Endgame*'s characters.

4. Charles Lyons, 'Beckett's *Endgame*: An Anti-Myth of Creation', *Modern Drama*, 7 (1964), 204–9.

5. Martin Esslin, *The Theatre of the Absurd* (Garden City, NY, 1961), p. 36.

6. Beckett, in a letter to Alan Schneider, 29 December 1957, in *Disjecta: Miscellaneous Writings and A Dramatic Fragment*, ed. Ruby Cohn (London, 1983), p. 109.

7. See, for example, Esslin, *The Theatre of the Absurd*, pp. 30–1 and Lyons, 'Beckett's *Endgame*'.

8. J. Huizinga, *Homo ludens* (Paris, 1951), pp. 29–31, 35, 176–7, 217.

9. B. S. Hammond, 'Beckett and Pinter: Towards the Grammar of the Absurd', *Journal of Beckett Studies*, 4 (1979), 37.

10. See Edith Kern, 'Samuel Beckett et les poches de Lemuel Gulliver', trans. Paul Rozenberg, *Revue des Lettres Modernes. Samuel Beckett: Configuration Critique, no. 8*, 100 (1964), pp. 69–81, for a discussion of the different world views implied by the treatment of objects such as eyeglasses in Swift or Beckett.

6

On the Dialectic of Closing and Opening in 'Endgame'

GABRIELE SCHWAB

Endgame is commonly ascribed to the theatre of the absurd. This categorisation has tended to determine the nature of interpretation by suggesting an understanding of the play as a symbolic representation of an absurd world. Thus we have been brought to see its characters as reduced subjects living in an alienated world of decay and awaiting death or an apocalypse with sick bodies and black humour. As a consequence, both the particularity and the peculiarity of the aesthetic presentation disappear from view and, accordingly, the crucial aesthetic experience as well: interpretation functions as closure. The 'absurd' becomes an ethnocentric category of remainders capable of accounting for everything which eludes either the familiar or the already understood.

What is it, then, in *Endgame* which seems so absurd? First impressions actually generate the suggestive fascination of an alien or exotic world. In a gloomy room, suffused with grey light, we meet the two main characters: Hamm in his wheelchair and Clov acting out a strange pantomime by trying to climb a ladder in order to look out the window. But why are the windows in this barren room so high? Did a taller race of men live here once? Or have the characters been shrinking? A picture also hangs in the room, but it is turned towards the wall. Does it symbolise the 'world upside-down?' In front we see two dustbins in which Hamm's parents, Nagg and Nell, vegetate. Is this more than a wicked metaphor for the generation gap?

The characters' most striking attribute is their advanced state of bodily deterioration. Clov is the only one who is still able to move, albeit with stiff knees. Nagg and Nell lost their legs in the famous bicycle accident in the Ardennes. Hamm is lame, blind and bleeding, needs tranquillisers and suffers from a chronic cough. All this is so highly suggestive of symbolic meaning that one can hardly evade the atmosphere of finality, decay and apocalypse. The characters themselves suggest that they might be the last survivors of a great disaster, and the lifelessness of the world outside supports this view. Nothing seems more evident than to see this scene as anticipating the advancing decay of our culture or an imminent global catastrophe.

Yet these interpretive closures lead us directly into the communicative dilemma in which *Endgame* quite openly and intentionally wants us to *be*. Those who limit themselves to such a reading miss the peculiar quality of the play which presents aesthetic strategies aimed at forestalling that gesture of closure which would construe the play as the symbolic representation of a deteriorating world. Whereas Samuel Beckett's own verdict, 'Beware of symbols!' is more than just a rhetorical warning against interpretive closures, the play's very atmosphere, its sensual imagery, and its mutilated plot lend themselves to such symbolic interpretations. What we find, in fact, is that the very invitation to 'misreadings' is one of the main communicative strategies. One cannot but be affected by the play's suggestive symbolism, especially when responding spontaneously. This conflict is crucial in the aesthetic response to Beckett's *Endgame*. We *ought* not to see any symbols, but find it impossible to see *none*. This communicative dilemma is responsible for the fact that the central (aesthetic) experience of the play is not anchored in referential meaning, but in the strategies guiding aesthetic response.

This displacement becomes most evident when one tries to hold on to one's notions of 'identity'. An audience whose expectations are still geared to characters having a circumscribed identity will be bitterly disappointed. The main characters, Hamm and Clov, don't seem to commit themselves to any psychic continuity as a basis for identity. To be sure, they display forms of behaviour and speech which resemble certain manifestations of an inner life. However, as soon as one attempts to assemble these manifestations into some coherent notion of personality, the characters shift to a different level of self-presentation.

If nothing else, it is at least possible to grasp the basic lines of kinship and relation: Hamm and Clov live their relationship on the model of master and slave. Nagg and Nell are Hamm's parents, and there are vague hints that Hamm might have adopted Clov as his son. But thinking in these terms becomes unreliable as soon as one realises that not only acting out but also playing with these roles proves to be Hamm and Clov's favourite preoccupation, if not obsession. In these games they relegate even the few palpable traits of identity to an iridescent half-light. The very notion of identity is revealed as a socially induced closure. In Hamm and Clov's playing with such roles the closure inherent in representations of identity is opened through never ending and continually variable substitutions. If *Endgame* brings to light the limits of totalisation, then it collapses the 'classical' relation to finitude with the modern one to 'play'. This collapse is possible because the characters' discourse lacks a centre which would be able to check and ground the play of substitutions[1] and thus to facilitate the representation of a centred subjectivity.

Doesn't Hamm himself, with his allusion to Zeno's heap of grain, play ironically with the viewer's search for an identity in the characters?[2] Hamm's ironic self-parody, his waiting for a heap to materialise out of the accumulation of discrete moments, a new quality that one might call life, resembles the spectator who attempts to compile an 'identity' for the characters out of ever new sequential repetitions and recursive speech. The audience might well take Hamm's grain paradigm as a hint that neither the identity of the characters nor the meaning of the play can be discovered by assembling fragments of identity or meaning. Perhaps, then, the audience could give up its search for neatly circumscribed wholes and instead, try to illuminate the iridescent plasticity of characters and play. This would also mean abandoning an interpretative gesture of closure in order to become involved in a decentring language-game of endless substitutions, that is, a game in which fragmented units of speech appear to be randomly substituted for each other. The play's language-game with the audience is reflected and mediated by the equally unfamiliar language-game of the characters. The latter contradicts not only all the expectations of dramatic dialogue, but also the very conditions for the functioning of dialogue. Neither is the dialogue situated in any intelligible context, nor does it derive from any representative function of speech or even a minimal amount of coherence. Moreover, it is full of contingencies, and these would be a stumbling block for any successful communication – at least according to systems theory.

Considering these disturbing qualities, one may be struck nonetheless by the easy flow of the dialogue. Most striking is the constant introduction of new topics, accompanied by the recurrence of nearly identical sequences of dialogue, though sometimes with the roles of the speakers reversed. The characters seem to be involved in a language-game, in which speech units can be moved around like chess pieces. There are not only identical but also unexpectedly abrupt moves in a game which functions according to rules unknown to the audience. An endless substitution of basic existential or anthropological problems seems to control the subject of conversation. The game, as it progresses with its preordained repetition of speech units, allows these themes to circle back on themselves. The content freezes into paradigmatic formulae belonging to an empty speech which the characters toss to and fro between them like a ball. One might think of it as a private use of language, which no longer requires one to mean what one says, but which gives one the freedom to play with the familiarity of old and empty rules. Or, from the perspective of the Derridean theory of closure: Hamm and Clov play with the superabundance of floating signifiers over and above all their possible signifieds in order to thematise the character of this surplus itself.

Yet this language game is also an end-game which focuses on ending and non-ending. Clov knows how to gain the advantage by threatening to violate the rules and terminate what is in principle an endless game. Or does even the threat of breaking the rules belong to the game? The nature of playing this game makes it impossible to identify the characters with their speech. By alternately exchanging slightly varied sequences of stereotyped dialogue in this game of substitution, the characters undermine any conceivable self-differentiation through their speech. So, for example, Clov's question, 'Why this farce, day after day?' has already been asked before by Nell; Hamm's 'Don't we laugh?' will in turn be taken up later by Clov.[3] Such a play with the substitution and repetition of speech units undercuts any notion of speech as reliable self-presentation.

To aggravate matters, the characters continually vacillate between different levels of play. Thus the boundaries between the 'endgame' and the 'games within the endgame' remain fluid. Moreover, Hamm caricatures our expectation that dramatic characters display some presentation of self. He parodies this function of self-presentation and self-ironically unmasks the seduction of the other through self-stylisation. By playfully enclosing himself in the role of a narcissistic artist, he discloses self-presentation as a mock fight for recognition.

His dependence on Clov as spectator caricatures, in addition, self-presentation as a way of performing for the internalised Other. Such a self-presentation can only portray a fictional self. One need only think of the scenes in which Hamm repeatedly urges Clov to ask him for his story, whereupon Clov immediately stages himself as a character who complies with this request.

How can a spectator react to these language games if they are not played by conventional rules and defy all our interpretive closures? As the characters refuse self-presentation and even caricature the latent function of self-presentation inherent in our speech, we become unsure of our relation to them. Where are the characters in their own speech? They don't seem to share our norms of communication. Their dialogue lacks representative qualities and hardly makes 'sense' to us. Whatever has the appearance of identity, representation or meaning is counteracted or contradicted in the course of the play. *The pervasive structure of negation and contradiction frustrates all partial investments of meaning and thereby fundamentally impedes every gesture of interpretation which strives for closure.*

Hamm and Clov present their dialogue as an imaginary game, replete with suggestive symbolism, yet without pretensions to any latent meaning. Thus they hedge themselves against any interpretation bent on deciphering a truth or centring the decentred play.[4] This strategy lures the audience into a type of double bind:[5] highly connotative 'symbols' suggest a latent dimension and invite ever newer constructions of meaning – apparently only to dismantle them as soon as they tend to stabilise. *Each invitation to closure is followed by new openings which prove that closure to be reductive.* It seems as if *Endgame* doesn't allow for the construction of latent meaning or as if the invitations to closure are intentionally set up as traps. The dilemma becomes inescapable: in order to 'understand' the characters, the audience must construe the symbolic meaning which the characters seem to suggest but, in fact, later reject. Should the audience do so, it is sanctioned, for the characters deride this meaning as a conventional projection of preconceived ideas:

> **Hamm** Clov?
> **Clov** (*impatiently*) What is it?
> **Hamm** We're not beginning to ... to ... mean something?
> **Clov** Mean something! You and I, mean something! (*Brief laugh.*) Ah that's a good one!

> **Hamm** I wonder. (*Pause.*) Imagine if a rational being came back to
> earth, wouldn't he be liable to get ideas into his head if he observed
> us long enough. (*Voice of rational being.*) Ah, good, now I see what
> it is, yes, now I understand what they're at! (*Clov starts, drops the
> telescope and begins to scratch his belly with both hands.*)[6]

The dynamic outlined here between a continual invitation to
closure and renewed opening can be seen as one of the play's central
strategic devices. It is anchored not only in what the characters say
but also in the structure of the play and the dramatic language. The
very act of symbolic interpretation, then, is being rejected as an
unacceptable closure of the play's open structure.

At first glance we seem to be offered a play decidedly rich in
connotation. Literary criticism has worked out allusions to literary
and cultural history which are sufficiently broad in scope: Hamm as
Hamlet, as 'ham' actor; his sheet as Christ's sudarium or a stage
curtain, and so forth. Nevertheless, such connotations cannot be
woven into the pattern of a coherent structure. The continual
fluctuation between offers of connotation and their withdrawal
prevents closure.

And yet, understanding that not even specific offers of connotation
refer to a hidden meaning already presupposes an involvement in the
play. Where closure is continually forestalled and connotations fail
to provide meaning, the audience will be excluded from its familiar
relation to language.

The different strategies enticing the audience into closures which
are subsequently rejected and reopened by the play lead to one
significant effect: they challenge language's 'structure of double
meaning'.[7] *Endgame* plays with the 'overabundance of signifier, in
relation to the signifieds'[8] in order, finally, to exaggerate altogether
the line between signifier and signified. This structure of double
meaning is, of course, fundamental to language in general. Its effect
is revealed as soon as a manifest meaning explicitly refers to a latent
one. Yet, if a play such as *Endgame* no longer carries an evident
manifest meaning, then we automatically suspect a latent one. While
this suspicion can be said to characterize our reaction to poetic
language in general, the challenge of *Endgame* consists in undermining this conventional receptive disposition. The failure of our efforts
to 'make sense' out of what we see by interpreting symbolically is –
from this point of view – the basic initial aesthetic experience of the
play. Thus both symbolic closure and its failure are the results of
textual strategies.

If we accept this, then the significance of the play can be found neither in the manifest nor in the latent dimension of dramatic speech. What I mean here is that significance is produced by dramatic speech but can no longer be bound to its meaning. It even tends towards an asemantic quality. Only when we forego our 'need for semantic succour'[9] in our construction of meaning can we grasp what the play is trying to convey and thus avoid projecting preconceived conventional 'meanings' and closures. Due to this shift in the reception process the main aesthetic potential of *Endgame* lies rather in the effect of that process than the substance of its imaginary stage world. The corresponding aesthetic strategy which consists in the rejection of the structure of double meaning, and the denial of closure produces very complex effects. It not only challenges the familiar relation between manifest and latent meaning, but also unsettles the audience's habits and conventions of communication. In the reception process we have to follow the play's strategy to let us shift between invitations to closure and required reopenings. Thus we may experience the extent to which our need for meaning induces us to close the gaps of the play by projecting our imaginations into them. This offers us some insight into our need for projective closures, as well as into the defensive qualities of our own communicative behaviour.

One main consequence of those strategies guiding audience response is that in the process of reception they shift our attention from the subjectivity of the fictional characters to our own subjectivity. What we then experience is our own decentredness. Since the structure of double meaning is the linguistic basis of decentred subjectivity, it is entirely appropriate that the play challenge this structure. The double meaning structure, i.e. a form of expression that can simultaneously show and hide meaning, gives us a chance not only to express, but also to react to, decentred subjectivity. Equally appropriate is the peculiar presentation of characters in *Endgame*. Decentred subjectivity is not conveyed by presenting 'decentred characters', but by challenging all familiar notions of subjectivity. To effect this challenge one cannot present so-called 'realistic' characters, but only highly stylised ones. Hamm and Clov are condensed and overdetermined characters. Similar to the figures who people our dreams, they have absorbed meanings, signs and properties from other characters as well as pure psychological or aesthetic functions. This complex and allusive overdetermination has occasioned numerous speculative interpretations.

Hamm and Clov have been seen as mythical characters in a mythical place or set within the tradition of the cosmological dialogue of the gods. They have been likened to Chronos and Mercury, to the sons of Noah after the flood, to Shakespeare's Hamlet, and also to Gloucester and Edgar in *King Lear*. Others have explicated the numerous echoes of other Beckett characters, Pozzo and Lucky in particular, as well as the Unnamable. On the other hand, *Endgame* has also been interpreted as an aesthetic differentiation of what is otherwise conceived of as a unity. Here the characters appear as components of a unified self or their room as a human brain whose various functions are divided up among the characters.

What is common to all of these interpretations is the desire to reduce the condensed form of the characters to a latent meaning. The symbolic connotations are, of course, the indisputable guides for a spontaneous response to the play. They ground the strategy of invitation to closure. The continual openings, however, prove those symbols to be irreducible. They resist any reduction to a latent meaning. Peter Brook characterises Beckett's peculiar way of using symbols: 'A true symbol is like Beckett's *Endgame*. The entire work is one *symbol* enclosing numerous others, though none of them are of the type which stand for something else; we get no further when we ask what they are supposed to mean, since here a symbol has become an object.'[10]

The condensation of characters constitutes still another device used to affect the audience's subjectivity. Condensations are gestalt formations unconsciously produced and invested with meaning. By appealing to our unconscious, then, the condensed characters of *Endgame* allow a different function of the communicative strategy to come into play: the transgression of the boundaries between consciousness and the unconscious. But in order to make the audience transgress these boundaries *Endgame* must pursue a double strategy. It takes into account decentredness by appealing on different levels and by different means to both conscious and unconscious domains of response.[11] Those aspects of the play which allow for immediate access are also those which invite interpretive closures. The central devices here are condensation and diffusion of meaning, both of which produce highly ambivalent appeals. Conscious annoyances are often counterbalanced by unconscious fascination. The latter becomes evident if we consider that the dissolution of the conventional symbolic functioning of language, which renders the process of understanding so difficult, also allows for effects which are normally absent or remain unconscious. Thus the strongest appeal and the most far-reaching effect of *Endgame* issue from what cannot be integrated into the symbolic order or cannot be centred; for example, speech acts violating the symbolic order of language, dramatic elements which cannot be integrated into the plot, behaviours which cannot be centred in the characters. In turn, this decentring affects the audience. The relative security of our status as audience allows us to be drawn into the game Beckett's characters are playing. But in so doing, we become temporarily infected by their decentred condition. Hamm and Clov play their identity games above all with the audience's identity, making it experience both its own decentredness and its need for centring interpretations and closures.

The strongest impulse for the reflective side of the aesthetic experience of *Endgame* comes from the strategy of continual opening by means of rejection and frustration. However fascinating these openings may unconsciously be, they must nonetheless be coped with consciously, for they are responsible for the continual failure of our attempts at interpretation. The history of Beckett criticism proves how difficult such an experience is even in terms of aesthetics. Thus it could also be viewed as the history of a collective defence against this failure, which in turn has given rise to a Beckett industry virtually addicted to symbolic interpretation.

Coping positively rather than negatively with the continual rejection of interpretations and the opening up of closure leads the audience to reflect upon the character of such interpretive acts themselves. For as long as the audience does not bale out of the communicative situation which arises in the immediate experience of the text and its dialectic of closing and opening or attraction and frustration, it remains trapped in an aesthetic double bind. There are, however, a number of clues in the play indicating that the way to get out of the trap is by shifting to a metalevel and reflecting on one's own interpretive acts. This strategy involves implicit references to the audience's situation – references which, like the above quoted passage, explicitly deal with projection and closure. *The aesthetic devices are thus targeted to a self-reflection which is both a mastery of the frustrated spontaneous response as well as an insight into one's own acts in interpretation.* In addition to the emotive and unconscious effects on the audience, self-reflection, then, can also be considered one of the basic elements in the overall response to *Endgame*.

I would now like to summarise some of the main points concerning the strategies guiding aesthetic response. As we have seen, the dynamic between closures and openings in *Endgame* entangles the audience both in the game the characters are playing and in a network made up of its own projections of meaning. This dynamic, however, is only one of the dis-illusioning strategies, which aim at a type of metaunderstanding or, better yet, metaexperience of one's own communicative acts. The effect is to make the audience conscious of how it projects meaning. This allows it to experience its projections as an attempt to close and centre something inherently open and decentred. We might also call this effort a defence against the experience of otherness. At the same time the dis-illusioning strategies aim at altering our need for centring and closing open structures.

The subtlest and most far-reaching of these strategies is the 'withdrawal of double meaning', i.e. the play's insistence on rejecting latent meaning, which interestingly enough itself operates as a double strategy. The separation of conscious from unconscious appeals accounts for the fact that the spectators themselves are decentred subjects. The importance of this double strategy lies in allowing them to transgress the border between consciousness and the unconscious. As our decentred subjectivity depends on polarising these domains, transgressing the boundaries between them also affects our decentred condition. Seen in this way, *Fin de partie* – the *Endgame* – *becomes a game involving the limits of our own subjectivity*. In the reception process, the conventions characterising our subjectivity are temporarily suspended. It is little wonder that so many react to the play as if a taboo were being violated.

Ambivalence, then, is also an important aspect of the aesthetic experience of *Endgame*. Transgressing the line between consciousness and the unconscious is always fraught with ambivalence. It releases anxieties of distintegration, emptiness or inundation by the unconscious. Simultaneously, however, it can become a source of delight. We derive pleasure from our positive investment in that original, undifferentiated mode of being which has been forced by the reality principle to survive in the reserves set aside for alternative states of consciousness.

The transgressive quality of *Endgame* is perhaps best documented by the isolated laughter so typical during the performance of Beckett's plays. I see this laughter as an expression of unconscious understanding or reaction. The spectator signals by his laughter that the strangeness of *Endgame* is not so foreign to him after all. This laughter arises spontaneously at the threshold of an unconscious understanding of something which our consciousness does not allow to be understood. However impenetrable or uninterpretable the dramatic action may seem, the laughter indicates that there is indeed a hidden understanding beyond consciousness. This laughter itself subverts the boundaries of our subjectivity in a specific way, since it involves, like laughter in general, a temporary abandoning of our ego-limits. And this is, of course, precisely one of the effects which *Endgame* had set as its goal.

The seemingly insignificant spontaneous laughter physically anticipates a type of transgression which has become one of the hallmarks of aesthetic response to contemporary art. The conscious experience of a shift in, or an expansion of, the limits of our subjectivity is more painful and has provoked extremely defensive responses towards modern art. *Endgame* makes us aware that not only the open rejection of a work of art but also its 'centring' by interpretive closures can be such a defence. In order to be able to derive benefit from the play's potential transgressions, we must learn to renounce interpretive closures. *Endgame* challenges them in three ways: it rejects them, it activates our unconscious desire for dissolutions, and it counterbalances its own transgressive tendencies by making us shift to a metalevel. Thus it aims at expanding the boundaries of our consciousness in two directions: towards the unconscious and towards self-reflection. Simultaneously, however, our need for closure emerges, in the aesthetic experience of *Endgame*, as a function of our need for meaning. One historical function of Beckett's strategy guiding aesthetic response resides in the objective not simply to supplant this need with another, but instead to work on it and, in so doing, to activate our latent desire for openings. By its dialectical rendering of closure, *Endgame* marks a historically significant threshold beyond which we experience an important change in our dispositions and in the nature of our aesthetic response. Hence, this is really the main reason *Endgame* has become so successful as an 'endgame' which plays with the limits of our subjectivity.

From *Yale French Studies*, 67 (1984), 191–202. The translator is D. L. Selden.

NOTES

[Gabriele Schwab's essay on *Endgame*, which is a condensed version of the arguments to be found in her book, *Samuel Becketts Endspiel mit der Subjektivität* (*Samuel Beckett's Endgame With Subjectivity*), Stuttgart, 1981, first appeared in a special issue of the influential poststructuralist journal *Yale French Studies* on forms of closure in literary texts. It affiliates itself much more explicitly than other deconstructive accounts in this volume with the work of Jacques Derrida and in particular with Derrida's theory of the infinite play of language, a play which is nevertheless continually closed off or 'centred' by the ineradicable human need for fixity, identity and meaning. Gabriele Schwab conjoins with this a psychoanalytical account of the ways in which audiences and readers fixate upon, or are released from, centred meaning. Her essay argues that *Endgame* both draws the audience into making interpretative guesses and assumptions but also 'fundamentally impedes every gesture of interpretation which strives for closure'. In doing so, the play undermines not only meaning, but the possibility of coherent subjectivity as presently conceived. But, at the end of her essay, Schwab offers the viewer and reader a refuge which is rare in a deconstructive account. Through being made aware of its own desire for meaning, and the play's frustration of that desire, the audience of *Endgame* is hoisted into 'a self-reflection which is both a mastery of the frustrated spontaneous response as well as an insight into one's own acts in interpretation'. This therapeutic transcendence of the limits of the ego is signalled in laughter, which Schwab sees not as stifled and uncertain (as Wolfgang Iser does in his essay in this volume), but as the enactment of the ego's knowing acceptance of dissolution and indeterminacy. Ed.]

1. Jacques Derrida, 'Structure, Sign and Play in the Discourse of the Human Sciences', in *Writing and Difference*, trans. Alan Bass (London, 1978), pp. 278–9.

2. 'Moment upon moment, pattering down, like the millet grains of . . . [*he hesitates*] . . . that old Greek, and all life long you wait for that to mount up to a life', Samuel Beckett, *Endgame, followed by Act Without Words* (New York, 1958), p. 70.

3. Ibid., pp. 32 and 14; 11 and 29.

4. See Derrida, 'Structure, Sign, and Play in the Discourse of the Human Sciences', p. 292: 'The one seeks to decipher, dreams of deciphering, a truth or an origin. . .'

5. This is not to be understood metaphorically, but rather in the sense of concrete, irreconcilable directives which force the audience into a paradoxical situation: (1) You must construe meaning, (2) This is possible only by means of projection, (3) You must not project. Compare *Double-Bind: The Foundation of the Communicational Approach to the Family*, ed. C. E. Sluzki and D. C. Ransom (New York, 1976).

6. Beckett, *Endgame*, p. 32.

7. This term is used here in the way Paul Ricoeur uses 'La structure du double sens' ('The structure of double meaning') in his book on Freud, *De l'interprétation: Essai sur Freud* (Paris, 1965), pp. 13–63.

8. Claude Lévi-Strauss quoted by Derrida, in 'Structure, Sign, and Play in the Discourse of the Human Sciences', p. 289.

9. See Samuel Beckett, *Watt* (London, 1963), p. 79.

10. P. Brook, 'Mit Beckett leben', in *Materialen zu Becketts 'Endspiel'*, ed. Michael Haerdter (Frankfurt, 1968), p. 32 (my translation).

11. The complexity of this double strategy has to be somewhat simplified here. For a more detailed analysis see my book *Samuel Becketts Endspiel mit der Subjektivität: Entwurf einer Wirkungsästhetik des Modernen Theaters* (Stuttgart, 1981), pp. 105–25.

7

'Endgame': On the Play of Nature

SYLVIE DEBEVEC HENNING

Since *Endgame* was first produced in London in 1957, it has received far more critical attention than *Murphy* (though less than *Godot*). This is certainly owing at least in part to the vogue for the 'heroic' humanism of various quasi-philosophical trends of the day. For *Endgame* has often been read as an illustration of certain extremely popular themes, particularly the 'absurdity' of the cosmos and the 'meaninglessness' of human existence within it. This approach has unfortunately overshadowed other possibilities.

Two critics who have reacted strongly to the existentialist view, but from seemingly divergent perspectives, are Stanley Cavell and Theodor Adorno.[1] Rather than presenting *Endgame* as merely symptomatic of 'modern ontology', both treat the play as a critical response to this particular avatar of Western metaphysics. They see the entire (or almost entire) philosophical tradition as implicated in the play's eternally frustrated search for ultimate meaning. And both point in consequence to the possibility of interpreting *Endgame* as a philosophical satire, while nonetheless presenting its critique of the rationalist tradition in fairly negative terms.

Totally instrumental, Adorno argues, contemporary rationalism has suppressed the possibility of meaning by eliminating all traces of the non-conceptual, namely, the material, the temporal, the historical. Only pure logic – empty technique or form – remains. Reason has thus deprived itself of the means of reflection upon both 'what is' and itself. *Endgame* provides no solution, but works to stimulate the elaboration of a new theory capable of dealing critically with this irrationality or 'meaninglessness' of modern socio-economic reality. Where Adorno sees a challenge, however, Cavell discovers only an essential equivocation. He considers the play stuck between two equally destructive (and in his opinion equatable) possibilities; nihilism and the revaluation of values, with no exit in sight.[2]

Thus, each critic may in the end be doing more to confirm than to contest the dominant, humanist interpretation. Diverging from this view, I should like to argue that, by casting the satire in a specifically Menippean or carnivalised 'form', Beckett does suggest an alternative to the paralysing despair so often detected at the heart of the modern situation.

Historically, the carnivalesque has always co-existed alongside our sober rationalist tradition. It has, however, been increasingly confined and reduced. According to Bakhtin and others, an effort to control and ultimately to eliminate all that does not conform to the totalising (and not infrequently totalitarian) presumptions of our cultural heritage has been operative on a fundamental level within the historically predominant hermeneutic perspectives whether philosophical, religious, moral, scientific or literary.

For Beckett the task of creative thinking is now to conduct the search for 'a form that accommodates the mess' instead of repressing it through an excess of rationalist order. The carnivalised satire comes to the fore in this context as a means of playing out 'messy' relations such that the anxiety they engender may be engaged in a more positive manner. An affirmation of their vital importance within the relative structures of temporal existence is in fact basic to this phenomenon, in as much as carnivalisation normally involves an open confrontation between contending forces, above all between those that strive for a full, harmonious unification and those that contest this desire.[3]

In *Endgame*, as perhaps in all of Beckett's work, the text itself reproduces such a contest on several levels. In the explicit narrative, Hamm and Clov struggle to deny the indeterminacy of their 'messy' condition. Yet, it keeps returning to increase their anguish. At the same time, they endeavour to eradicate crucial aspects of the carnivalesque – the body, nature, time, history, laughter – whenever they manifest themselves. A similar act of double repression is repeated on the stylistic level, where an effort at straightforward monovocality and orderliness is countered by the processes of linguistic dissemination that cannot be contained. On all levels, the carnivalesque both counteracts the totalising impetus and interacts with it in an agon that contributes greatly to the palpable tension of the play. *Endgame* is largely a comment upon similar confrontations that have repeatedly occurred throughout the course of Western history. By the very act of testing and contesting our familiar teleological hermeneutics, moreover, the play may, in the uncertainty of its own nature, be demonstrating and providing, not simply a critique, but an alternative as well.

Let us suppose, then, that *Endgame* takes place within the mind: not that of an individual subject like Murphy, but that of Western culture itself, centred as it is upon the human subject. Its 'bare interior' is lit by a 'grey light', that is, neither the true Light nor total Darkness, but the half-light in between. Here, on a mental stage, the cultural mind will replay in perpetual frustration its various interpretations of life and world. What had been for Murphy a moment of 'Belacquan bliss' upon the threshold of purgatory has become for Hamm and Clov a dark night of longing at the gates of a paradise lost.

As often in the medieval theatre, the opening tableau is a concrete representation of the end of days. The exit from the prison cell – of life, of mind, of language itself – is through the door stage right. The characters who are living there *huis clos* always remain nonetheless within sight of the door. Their being there is lived toward a passage that they hope will lead to a better situation, or at least to a different one. They hope to transform their inevitable finitude from a 'simple' closure into a meaningful end.[4] Next to the door, however, there hangs a picture with its face to the wall, a traditional sign of mourning. Whose picture is it – the all-seeing deity of *Film*, the Old Boy of *Murphy*? Is the human mind in mourning after the death of that Being who created and gave meaning to the door, indeed, who was the Door?

The condition of Hamm and Clov might then be compared to what Pascal described as the 'misery of man without God'. He can be satisfied with nothing less than the infinite and absolutely stable, and so can find no real satisfaction at all. The characters' attempts to forestall the inevitable may thus be prompted by a fear that there might in fact be no fully meaningful end. The complexity of their perception of this improbable way out will in any case contribute to the passion of their play.

Of course, the door could also be a way in: into a new earthly paradise (or is it only a new hell?). With the disappearance of the deity, man is left to his own devices. He must find another authority to give his life direction and fulfil his Pascalian 'capacity for God', be it Reason, *Geist*, Will, the Natural 'Laws' of science, or a Transcendental Ego. These and other substitute centres are produced by thought which, by itself, Pascal too considered man's greatest attribute. When a man begins to search for a concept, or idea, to replace the divine Mind (*Mens*), it is accordingly not so surprising that he should find, sooner or later, himself. The new heaven becomes what it was already for Murphy: the human mind itself.[5]

On the left side of this opening tympanal tableau is a counterpart of the door, another way out (or in) as debris. The two dustbins standing there, like two funerary urns, are also signs of mourning, not for the heavenly Father, but for Hamm's own grotesquely earthbound parents. Like his (and man's) biblical ancestors, they are associated with the physical body. Man comes into life and departs from it as what *Murphy* called a 'waste product' of the organic processes: ashes to ashes, dust to dust. They may also be associated with the social body and all its 'organs': family, church, state. They evoke as well the historical body, including both the biological and the cultural heritage.

In both West and East, the physical body has normally been regarded as earthly detritus that corrupts the spirit and shackles its freedom (e.g. by Platonism and Christianity, but also by the Sartrean existential humanism in vogue at the time of *Endgame*). At best it is perceived together with the social dimension of life as a means to a higher (and therefore non-corporeal) end: as the tools of *Geist* or Proletarian Man on the dialectical march toward cultural self-realisation. In positivism (including important aspects of the Marxist perspective) it functions as the mere object of scientific law. And when even this instrumental value was cast into doubt, organic life became, as it was for certain prominent forms of religion, simple refuse. In one way or another, by either assimilation or elimination, nature is mastered and its most 'earth-bound' elements depreciated, deprecated, and finally denied.

Between the two extremes is Hamm, seated in his Faustian chair on castors, a pose that both repeats and varies that of Murphy, Mr Kelly, Molloy, Moran, the Unnamable *et al.* Hamm as man (*homme*), man as soul (*âme*). Blind to the sensory world, his body immobilised, Hamm is man reduced, in metaphysical terms, to his most essential features: those of the mind or soul. At the centre of this 'theatre of the world', he occupies a place of authority, with the power to separate the damned from the saved, the power of a man-God upon his mercyseat.

This centre, however, is double. Beside Hamm stands Clov, his alter ego. Clov reminds us that man is by nature dual, both matter and spirit. Hamm and Clov might together represent man, the former as mind, the latter as body. Yet to be Clov(e) is already to be two, and not simply two, but simultaneously simple and dual. Even from within the Christian or classical framework, Clov, as man's material nature, would not be totally devoid of spiritual qualities himself. Although inferior or even hostile to spirit, matter is still regarded as part of divine creation.

Traditional metaphysics does, all the same, effectively bind one leg of the Clov(e). Reduced to the instinctual, that which is cloven represents all that is infernally 'sinful' in man. Or his more material functions may be so tightly governed by 'natural' reason and law that he is progressively crippled. In the idealist tradition (and some consider all of Western philosophy fundamentally idealist), the material leg is all but amputated, leaving only spirit to represent nature as a whole, at least in its 'essence'. To deprive the Clov(e) of its most corporeal member, however, is in a sense to destroy it.[6]

Not only is Clov cloven, he is also 'in' Hamm, as Hamm is 'in' him. Hamm himself is a form of Clov, albeit a more repressed and therefore enfeebled one. Man may be soul, but he is also flesh (ham). And the soul (*anima*), as mediator between pure spirit and pure matter, is also double. A portion (*mens*) participates in the divine intellect, while another (*animus*) experiences the sensory world. This problematically cloven nature has been a major thorn in the side of our classical-Christian anthropology. And it cannot be removed. Beside Hamm stands perpetually this devilish supplement: too material to be totally assimilated, too spiritual to be completely eliminated.

That which is cloven is fundamentally undecidable. It cannot be reduced to one leg or another of the complex relations of sameness with difference that it embodies. Nor does it 'amount to' their totality. The problematic, impure 'gap' in between is never quite closed, nor ever extensive enough to become a complete break. The cloven situation is therefore liminal, yet agonistic both in itself and with regard to the familiar 'home' oppositions (matter/spirit, body/mind, object/subject, nature/culture, other/self, and so on), at once more reminiscent, more promising, of unification and less open than

they to attainment of that end, a perpetual cleaving to and simul-
taneous cleaving asunder. The cloven thus engages the problem or
process of *différance.* It is subject not to ultimate solutions but to
modified repetitions and more or less successful accommodations. It
points in this respect to the ancient but ongoing interaction of
repression and displacement within our cultural context.[7]

It is Clov, this perplexing supplementary excrescence at the side of
the central One, who sets the play in motion. For Plotinus, such an
originary excess implied an overflow of limits that was also an
expulsion, a casting out of that which cannot (or can no longer) be
contained within the whole. It is, in sum, a form of cleaving and thus
an act by 'Clov'. Clov sets the play in motion by breaking away from
Hamm and setting off upon his own eccentric path. Yet, to cleave in
this way would only be to obscure or even to destroy the nature of
the cleft. The 'end' of Clov's action appears to be the end of the
cloven itself. He is the agent, in some sense, of his own eventual
elimination.

In the beginning of the play there is not the word but the deed, a
rather Faustian notion. Or rather, the act – for Clov's activity is part
of a routine, even a conventional comic routine. In the beginning,
then, there is already both repetition and, in a sense, the act of
interpretation. And here it is also an act of repression. The 'beginning' (of the play, of the world, of civilisation and culture) is thus
marked by an effort to control the originary indeterminacy of
(man's) nature. It is even the nature of/in man that is repressed.
Thereafter, Clov will only repeat and intensify this attempt to cleave
fully asunder.

What his act accomplishes amounts to a final uncovering of
Hamm. Man, after the exclusive deed that establishes and maintains
the dominant intellectual tradition (viz., the separation of mind from
matter)[8] is himself reductively reconstituted in a spiritual mode, as
soul. Physically, he is blind, paralysed, moribund.

On his way out the door, Clov can therefore stop to announce that
the process of repression has reached its culmination. To be finished
– perfect and closed – is in this case to be soul alone, without the
body, man without his cloven nature. It is fitting, then, that Clov as
he leaves should repeat 'Christ's Parthian shaft'.

The first spoken word of the play is also '*fini*' indicating finality, in
the sense both of finite and finished, and pointing therefore to the
problem of teleology right from the start. It is a significant, albeit
uncertain beginning. For what precedes the 'word', on stage and in

the text, cannot be dismissed as meaningless chaos, while teleology is at the same time the most obvious issue addressed by *Endgame*.

What exactly is implied in this statement, 'It is finished'? Among other things, that one has, as Hegel observed, already placed oneself, in some (hyperbolic) sense, beyond finality and, paradoxically, become able to look back upon it. It is consequently a moment that, by exceeding its own goal, renders questionable the latter's status as *telos*.

Even the very simple grammatical structure of Clov's statement, like Murphy's expression of self-identity, reaffirms the notions of time, space and movement, all of which dispute the finished, thinglike quality of that putative end in itself.[9] The reified state that Clov posits with his initial 'finished' slips away even as he appears to grasp it: 'Nearly finished, it must be nearly finished' ['It will perhaps finish'].[10]

Clov's opening sentences fall from his lips like the grains of 'that old Greek' (Is it Zeno or Eubulides?), indicating 'the impossible heap': a plurality of separate moments will never make a whole.[11] Clov transforms the pain of being 'imperfect' into a sense of guilt at having fallen from a static state ('finished') into the indeterminacy of time ('it will perhaps finish'). Unable ever to atone for this 'sin', he is condemned, like Sisyphus or Ixion, to perpetual frustration. 'I can't be punished any more.'

What is finishing will never be made clear. Indeed, the characters remain incapable of defining it, naming it, giving it an identity. In order to bring 'it' to an end, the troublesome aspects ('*ça*') would have to disappear and be replaced by something completely knowable. There is no room for the undecidable in any perfect state, be it a republic, absolute knowledge, the well-adjusted psyche, or 'ordinary language'.[12]

Clov's response to this inconclusiveness is to retreat into a refuge of his own, analogous in its symmetry to the New Jerusalem. The door, we are told, leads into the kitchen. Now a kitchen, it is true, is a sort of domestic laboratory in which the old Greeks prepared their coction – the same coction they also associated with their ideal of balance, equilibrium, and harmonious proportions (cf. *Murphy*). Nevertheless, a kitchen maintains a strong relation to the bodily realm. Like the City of God Saloon, therefore, Clov's refuge is not without its carnivalesque dimensions. His kitchen is not so far from the garbage cans as he would like to believe. ...

Toward nature in general Hamm and Clov display attitudes that are complex and fraught with contradiction, if not outright confusion. For Hamm, who can only speculate upon the scanty evidence provided by his 'pupil', nature appears as constant change, understood in entropic terms. He only regrets that he and Clov do not seem to be part of it: 'Nature has forgotten us' (*E* 11). For Clov, their own deterioration proves that this is not the case. They are part of the natural process, but that process requires disintegration. In nature there is no gain without loss; indeed, everything is eventually lost. Every natural being is in time left behind as detritus. Disappointed, Hamm acquires a more simply negative, and even destructive, view of nature. If there is neither absolute gain, nor anything free of change (and therefore of loss), better that the natural process should not exist at all. Hamm, however, refuses to acknowledge the nihilistic implications when they are actually voiced by Clov: 'You exaggerate' (*E* 11). Sobriety, as Adorno observes, is one proven means of sabotaging thought, and by this means Hamm manages to blind himself even further.[13]

Clov, on the other hand, would limit his knowledge of nature to what can be generalised systematically from observation, objective and precise, of his environment. The result is a devitalisation of nature through reduction to abstract terms. A desire for domination through scientific knowledge, the humanist form of what Claude Lévi-Strauss calls 'species imperialism', may thus conceal a desire to eliminate nature altogether: 'There's no more nature' (*E* 11).[14]

Awareness of the fact that the object of their study is subject to continued modifications and variations causes both characters considerable distress. Their efforts to comprehend and explain the natural world repeatedly go awry, generating a mass of fairly obvious distortions. 'No one that ever lived ever thought so crooked as we' (*E* 11). Yet Hamm and Clov do not resort to critical reflection upon the way such problems have habitually been addressed. The one looks to control his anxiety with tranquillisers, while the other retreats into his cubicle. Both are growing impatient with the entire interpretative project: 'This is slow work' (*E* 12). Clearly, it is not leading very quickly toward a final resolution.

That does not mean it is leading nowhere, however. The dialogue continues. From the problem of nature, we pass to that of knowledge. The kitchen, from Hamm's point of view, is not unlike Plato's cave. Like the chained prisoners in the latter, Clov passes his time there staring at the wall. Hamm offers two mocking descriptions of what Clov sees. 'Mene. Mene', suggests that if Clov believes he can comprehend the world in numerical or quantitative terms, he is undoubtedly mistaken (*E* 12).[15] More importantly, Hamm appears to be suggesting that strictly quantitative methods involve something analogous to faith in a revelation.

The great pioneer scientists were all serenely confident of the mathematical (and therefore abstract) simplicity of nature. To them it was not merely a methodologically necessary premise; it was a fundamental fact of the universe. Galileo believed that mathematics best represents the structure of the natural world. Whatever can be expressed in mathematical discourse is true, and God himself could have no clearer knowledge of the natural order it comprehends.

When Bacon took over and modified Plato's cave image, he incorporated it within a metaphoric complex, a portion of which could be turned against Plato himself. The philosopher's dependence upon deductive reasoning *a priori* and the ideal of pure mathematics were included among the 'idols' that lead to erroneous conclusions.

Following Bacon, much empiricism continued, in Heine's words, to 'run about sniffing at things, to collect and classify their characteristics', until Kant appeared. Taking up the cave metaphor once again, Heine concludes: 'Kant proved that we knew nothing of things as they are in and for themselves and that we can have no knowledge of them except as far as they are reflected in our own soul.'[16] Thus, in helping to re-establish the possibility of science in the wake of Hume, Kant also sought to establish its fundamentally subjective limits. Scientific knowledge could henceforth be predicated upon the existence of certain basic categories and procedures of the human mind. One could no longer hold any act of perception to be completely objective, an unmediated vision of the world as it really is. Kant attempted to describe the conditions of the cave and to refute Plato's conviction that science can provide a way out.

Hamm, then, who would mock Clov by pointing out their differences, has at the same time uncovered similarities. Clov too is 'dreaming' when he takes his empirical observations for a straightforward image of the real world. Hamm's ironic description of Clov's activity simultaneously obscures and calls attention to the fact. Clov peers at 'naked' bodies: a crude and vulgar sort of knowledge deriving from a mode of viewing that remains necessarily improper. Clov appears at times to realise that he is interpreting and experiences the waning of his confidence in the absolute status of scientific knowledge: 'I see my light dying' (*E* 12). With his greater degree of self-consciousness, Hamm would even now retain superiority. How can Clov, whom he cynically calls his 'dog', possess any light of his own? Is not Hamm the ultimate source of Clov's illumination? Is not his decline therefore more significant? 'Take a look at me and then come back and tell me what you think of *your* light' (*E* 12).

The impotence behind Hamm's aggressive posture renders him incapable of genuine domination. On the other hand, his persistent arrogance makes harmonious relations difficult. He tries again by returning to the problem of nature. What of Clov's grain? If an increasing heap cannot make a mathematical whole, perhaps a sprouting pile can make an organic one. Hamm would still believe that, in the world's vast seedbed, physical change is evidence that a larger, metaphysical Force is working itself out in time toward self-realisation. Clov, however, has no faith in any such teleological design: 'They'll never sprout!' (*E* 13).

Is it impossible, then, to understand what is happening? Can we ascribe no meaning to change and to the passage of time? An inability to comprehend it all by means of a rationally totalised scheme is a source of Hamm's anguish, an anguish that Clov does not appear to share. The latter merely concludes that 'something is taking its course', believing he has made an impartial, objective statement (*E* 13). He cannot of course know that there is such a 'thing' or that it has any 'course' to follow. Moreover, he too still dreams of abstracting a final all-encompassing system: 'I love order. It's my dream. A world where all would be silent and still and each thing in its last place, under the last dust' (*E* 57).

Thus even if he at times openly disdains Hamm's desperate desire for meaningful purpose, Clov too aspires to full comprehension. In itself a perfect whole, the world would not need – it could not have – any other purpose or end. Traditionally, in fact, the fully self-consistent, unified system is its proper *telos*. The fact that his 'dream' rests upon a network of conventional presuppositions, and not upon inductive conclusions from sensory experience, creates another similarity between the speculative Hamm and the ostensibly more empirical Clov.

Clov's somewhat reluctant accommodation to teleology is enough to bring temporary agreement while advancing the dialogue to another stage. Having 'met', like Miss Counihan, Neary and Wylie, the two characters can now separate, Hamm pretending to expel Clov, Clov pretending to leave freely. 'We're getting on' (*E* 14).

Once each has withdrawn into his own abstract dreamworld, the refuse they have left behind comes to life. Nell and Nagg emerge from their garbage cans to replay the dialogue between spirit and matter in a more organic mode. Like the most problematic element of a dream, the cloven is repeated and varied, now condensed into composite figures, now dispersed into manifold manifestations. These displacements are not unrelated to the act of repression. Concealed or occluded in one form, the repressed element always returns in another.

First Nell and Nagg attempt to consummate a union. *'Their heads strain towards each other, fail to meet, fall apart again'* (E 14). Why do they continue this comedy of frustrated conjugal love? Perhaps for the same reason they daily remember their tandem accident and catalogue their losses. In a manner reminiscent of Clov's opening act, they would deaden the pain by recasting it as a vaudeville routine. They too would master anxiety by compulsively repeating the actions that provoke it. Beginning again, this anxious play again begins with an act of repetition.

The bicycle accident outside Sedan in which Nell and Nagg lost their 'legs' might be described as a carnivalised condensation of Taine's catastrophic history of modern France: from Enlightenment through Revolution to the final impotence of Napoleon III. The tandem alignment of classical spirit and a belief in scientific progress set up human reason in the driver's seat of civilisation, but only by first depriving mankind of its historical sense. 'Deprived of [its] precious legacy [*legs*]', the nation succumbed to Rousseau's call for a return to 'nature'.[17] The significance of Nell and Nagg may thus have less to do with what Georg Lukács saw as Beckett's doctrine of bestial irrationalism,[18] than it does with a criticism of our smugly rationalist tradition for its inclination toward something analogous to precisely that sort of reduction. The fact that Beckett may also be having critical fun with Taine's quasi-castration theory does not by itself invalidate this line of interpretation.

The resurgence of the corporeal Nell and Nagg keeps Hamm from mental peace within himself. In good Freudian fashion, their burlesque intercourse may remind him of a childhood scene when he, like his Old Testament namesake, beheld, as it were, the means by which he was conceived.[19] For his transgression Noah's son was cursed. Nagg's son curses his father for the latter's original sin of the flesh: 'Accursed fornicator' (E 10).

To displace the distressing primal scene, Hamm attempts an imaginary re-creation of the sensory world he has denied. Like Fichte he would derive the objective 'Not-I' from the purely spiritual 'I'. Nagg finds it a ludicrous enterprise. His own world – that of the bodily desires that require satisfaction, of the mange that needs to be scratched – is for him the true world. Nagg therefore counters Hamm with a materialist reworking of the mental re-creation myth: 'the world and the trousers' (*E* 22–3).

The comparison calls to mind Herr Teufelsdröckh's magnum opus. Nagg, however, presents the Divine Tailor as a careless craftsman who rushed through the job in order to rest on the Sabbath: *Genesis* as a bad Jewish joke. In recent decades it has been the absurdists who have, with a sort of arrogance, regarded the cosmos as 'botched'. Yet, the idea has a long genealogy. In Nagg's burlesque rendition the human tailor, by working from Christmas to Easter, manages to save his creation, but only by concealing 'the hollow' beneath the smoothly tailored lines of an artificial bottom: a humanist, and to some extent existentialist, rewriting of a bad Christian joke.

Nell too is obsessed by the bottom: in this case the bottom of Lake Como, that draws her down to the depths of nostalgic reverie: 'It was deep, deep. And you could see down to the bottom. So white. So clean' (*E* 21). Her own retreat from materiality involves an act of negation, of 'nelling'. Hers is the death knell of the body that longs for a return to the more basic, more nearly static condition of the inorganic world. Here too the desire for the bottom is ultimately a desire for the end. More overtly corporeal than either Hamm or Clov, Nell and Nagg nevertheless suggest still other ways of either overcoming or undermining the life of the flesh: 'By rights we should have been drowned' (*E* 21). Nell's negativity, however, is more profound. The dull, gnawing pain of living is too much a part of Nagg for him to give it up.

The couple's continual prattle, so similar to his own conversations with Clov, disturbs Hamm's solipsistic dreaming. It draws attention to his residual facticity, those nagging remains of 'Not-I': physical aspects, his heredity, his past in general. And therefore to their, his and 'its' imperfection: 'Will this [*ça*] never finish' (*E* 23). All must be expelled and carted away. Hamm's putative self-sufficiency is lost if he cannot rid himself of that which limits his spiritual freedom: 'My kingdom for a nightman! ... Clear away this muck!' (*E* 23).[20] This is, as usual, a job for Clov.

Fundamentally, however, it is Nell's own nihilism that explains her demise. If her mortal itch stops ('She has no pulse [*pouls/poux*]' –

E 23), it is not really because of any power Hamm might have, whatever he might say. ('Oh for that my powder is formidable' – phrase eliminated from the English version – *FP* 39, my translation.) Her existence was 'bottled' before Clov put the lid on her.

Hamm and Clov seem more reluctant to cut all the ties that bind them in material ways to a more vital existence. Rather than take responsibility for freely willing his end, Clov would prefer it be determined for him. For example, he restates as exile – 'She told me to go away, into the desert' – Nell's dying exhortation – 'Desert' (*E* 23). And Hamm refrains from permanently obstructing Nagg's re-emergence. The psychologically related decision to postpone elimi-nating his own bodily waste would, on the other hand, be physio-logically counter-productive in the end.

His subsequent efforts to circumscribe the limits of his domain belong to this complex of retentive inclinations, for it promises to give Hamm a surer comprehension of his powers vis-à-vis the physical world. Can he eliminate it entirely or must he struggle merely to dominate and thus control it? The walls mark his limits and they embody the basic building blocks of modern epistemology: space, time, number, causality, and so on.

Like the philosopher in the 'Preface' to Nietzsche's *Twilight of the Idols*, Hamm would sound out these fundamental concepts. 'Do you hear? (*He strikes the wall with his knuckles.*) Do you hear? Hollow bricks! (*He strikes again.*)'

What if the bricks were, as Hume suggested, merely the products in the mind of mere perceptual habit? Or what if they represented the innate mental categories with which Kant responded in an attempt to describe the *a priori* conditions of legitimate scientific rationality? Hamm's wall would then resemble Clov's cave. What happens if these categories are themselves understood as interpretation rather than pure truth? If 'all that's hollow' (*E* 26), then at the limit one would be thrown back. The dream of a full comprehension remains unfulfilled: 'That's enough. Back!' 'We haven't done the round' (*E* 26). But need this imply that all is devoid of meaning?

Reduced to the hollow, both here and in Nagg's joke, the 'cleft' now reappears thwarting anew the desire to rebuild the world on an absolute foundation. Hamm would fill it himself. Yet, he relies upon Clov to place him at the centre and must continue to endure the troubling proximity of this all too necessary adjunct.

Hamm senses that the security of his own small domain might be enhanced through nihilation of the outside world. His authority, however, ought not to depend upon any empirical evidence of it. Clov's (Galilean) telescope ought only to confirm Hamm's speculative insight. Clov himself eventually objects to the way it is used to maintain him in a position of subservience. Even the most accurate observation, however, is inadequate by itself. True knowledge requires what Bacon describes as a methodological 'ladder'. Hamm's displeasure at the thought – 'I don't like that' (*E* 28) – derives in part from a suspicion that his assistant would thus acquire the means of displacing the master. A Baconian Clov might succeed in uniting the rational and empirical aspects of knowledge rather like a Hamm cured of his sensory blindness.

Indeed, the prevailing tendency of Western science has traditionally been to seek after that coordination of observation and method that would enable mankind at last to comprehend the world as a systematic whole. With Clov this excess of expended energy turns into a comic routine: '*Exit Clov with telescope. . . . Enter Clov with ladder, but without telescope. . . . He sets down ladder under window right, gets up on it, realises he has not the telescope, gets down. . . . He goes towards door. . . . Exit Clov. . . . Enter Clov with telescope. He goes toward ladder. He gets up on ladder, raises the telescope, lets it fall*' (*E* 28–9). Yet, modern physics has been no more successful than Comtian positivism in achieving Bacon's Great Instauration that many, if not all, men of science still seem to desire.

In a moment of self-conscious theatricality, Clov decides to gauge the reaction of the audience: '(*He gets down, picks up the telescope, turns it on auditorium.*) I see . . . a multitude. . . . in transports.' (The French version reads simply 'en delire': delirium, in a frenzy – *FP* 45. The English specifies 'in transports . . . of joy' – *E* 29.) No one in the theatre finds this joke amusing, but its 'serious' dimension need not be simply negative. A public that accepts uncritically the propositions of a conventional science – propositions emanating in good part from principles, or impulses that are fundamentally hostile to its own material existence – is delirious, if not mad.

In *Dialectic of Enlightenment*, Max Horkheimer and Theodor Adorno seek to demonstrate that Baconian scientific and technological enthusiasm, with its ethos of instrumentalism and exploitation, contributes importantly to the alienation and repressive standardisation of modern society. Heidegger, following Nietzsche, goes further, arguing that both rationalism and positivistic empiricism belong to the same metaphysical, hence fundamentally anti-natural, tradition. Clov is accordingly right to stress the farsightedness ('*longue vue*' –

FP 45) of those who have attempted to see through the popular delusion.

Clov's seriocomic self-parody – 'I did it on purpose' (*E* 29) – thus suggests the insufficiencies of his own habitual procedures. His playfulness also helps to recover the possibility of a different sort of science, one that displaces the desire for systematic unification and technological mastery of the world in favour of a renewed openness to nature and its capacity for continual (self-)contestation, a transformation, but also a restoration, of science: 'Things are livening up.' Is this a serious proposition? 'Well? Don't we laugh? . . . I don't. . . . Nor I' (*E* 29). . . .

For Hamm and Clov the game of life acquires true significance only in so far as it can be described in terms of a comprehensive system or goal. Like the all too Sartrean hero of *Nausea*, they are faced with the fundamental problem of excess and lack. On the one hand, the characters are unable to provide an interpretation that is fully adequate to empirical reality. In one way or another, life seems constantly to go beyond total conceptual comprehension. On the other hand, their desire for perfect order and propriety may itself become excessive. The world is then inadequate to their expectations. In both cases, the characters take their own desires and aspirations as the measure of all things. This is what authorises existentialist interpretations of *Endgame*.

I am not, then, trying to argue that they are irrelevant to the play, but that their relevance is of a different sort than the predominant view of Beckett would allow. Existentialist humanism, I have tried to show, is itself critically situated within the play and cannot, therefore, provide a complete explanation of it. To deny or overestimate the significance of Beckett's relation to the Cartesian *cogito*, or human subjectivity in general, would be difficult. It forms one of the more prominent departure points in most, if not all, his fictional and non-fictional work. His 'subjects' are usually engaged in endless struggles with the more or less irrational 'others' that constitute their natural world. By repeatedly destabilising the various anthropocentic structures that the subject erects, these natural forces continually frustrate the desire for rational mastery.

Yet, regret or despair at disorderly conduct of the world is not the 'essential meaning' or 'message' of Beckett's own 'play'. It is merely one tempting response to the situation – a response, however, his work normally treats in a demonstratively critical, or at least parodic, fashion. *Endgame* is typical in this respect. Indeed, Beckett's writing tends forcefully to convey the impression that humanism, including its existentialist variant, has exaggerated the extent of our freedom, the nature of its relation to human subjectivity, and the degree of dignity which the latter has granted him.[21]

Endgame suggests ways in which humanist ideology may actually have debased mankind along with the entire natural world to which we inevitably belong. Both the 'idealist' Hamm and the more 'technocratic' Clov desire a simpler, a neater, and less troublesome world, a world in which comprehension can be related to security through one-sided processes of domination and control. It is a desire rooted in humanist – and at bottom, other-worldly – ideas about man and his relation to all non-human beings. Beckett's play may thus imply that human dignity would be enhanced if *homo rationalis* were to see himself less as master of the world, the focus of its meaning and value, than as one vital element in a decentred world that can never be securely placed under the dominion of any.[22] ...

Those who long for a secure universe, completely under control, at least cognitively, are not always inclined to waver under the impact of the doubts aroused by recent developments in science and philosophy. Every possibility that does not conform to traditional modes of apprehension, or at least hold out the hope of satisfying the desire for a familiar idea of good order, then appears in a threatening light. It upsets and may well destroy the fragile 'perfection' of the various models they employ. What modern science has come increasingly to think of as an inherent degree of relative insecurity in the universe, a universe in which man participates as a vital, but no longer central, element implies, however, that the carnivalesque with its proliferation of grotesque 'forms' need not be evaluated simply in terms of its destabilising potential. Indeed, destabilisation itself need not be taken simply as a threat to every form of order.

The absence of a unique, ultimate meaning is open, I think, to another interpretation, one that regards it with less apprehension, regret and gloom. In this case, the demise of the one implies not chaos or significative void, but a virtual cornucopia of relative or partial forms, meanings and values. Beckett's seemingly fragmented and dispersed cultural references then become a network of signifying elements that never coalesce into a total interpretation, but are not on that account devoid of all significance. This understanding of regulated interpretive play would contribute to the possibility of new structures of meaning more open to self-contestation and for that reason better able to withstand the anxiety and internal pressures that have contributed to the breakdown of older, more repressively humanist ones.[23]

From Sylvie Debevec Henning, *Beckett's Critical Complicity: Carnival, Contestation and Tradition* (Lexington, 1988), pp. 86–93, 97–106, 115–17, 121.

NOTES

[Sylvie Debevec Henning's essay is taken from the chapter on *Endgame* in her book *Beckett's Critical Complicity*. The book as a whole argues that Beckett's work stands in a relation of 'critical complicity' to Western philosophical traditions in the way it simultaneously extends and undermines philosophical themes and preoccupations. The particular focus in this discussion is the attitude towards nature taken in *Endgame*. Henning argues that the play enacts a breakdown of the dualisms of subject and object, soul and body, knowledge and the senses, which have been so dominant within Western philosophy. The result of this is a collapse of the authority of the knowing subject, who, like Hamm, is unable any more to exercise its dominion over a crumbling but still recalcitrant universe. But this collapse may also have positive possibilities, in both philosophical and political senses, for it may open up the possibility of a form of knowledge which is not based upon a separation from and disavowal of the body and of nature in general. In subjecting abstract reason to this kind of critique, Beckett's work might almost be said to be part of an 'ecological' attempt to meditate upon the modes of human inherence in the natural world rather than reducing that world to the status of object. Ed.]

1. Stanley Cavell, 'Ending the Waiting Game: A Reading of Beckett's *Endgame*', in *Must We Mean What We Say?: A Book of Essays* (New York, 1969), pp. 115–62. Theodor Adorno, 'Towards an Understanding of *Endgame*', trans. Samuel Weber, in *Twentieth-Century Interpretations of 'Endgame': A Collection of Critical Essays*, ed. Bell Gale Chevigny (Englewood Cliffs, NJ, 1969), pp. 82–114.

2. Cavell proposes a means for escaping from 'equivocation', ibid., p. 143. It derives from his conception of ordinary language, and in particular from what his discussion of *Endgame* regards as its capacity for conveying necessary implications, extralogical in nature yet 'perfectly comprehensible to anyone who can speak' (p. 123). Within the bounds of this linguistic republic, whose natives all intuitively obey the laws of their common language, true disagreement simply cannot persist. Full meaning resides, then, not in some 'transcendent' realm, but in the communal experience of the shared Logos. The problem with this

approach is not just that it is, after all, less innovative than Cavell believes. It also has unrealistically, unnecessarily, restrictive 'implications' for the interpretation of complex literary works such as *Endgame*. If all native speakers have innate or *a priori* understanding of the connotations implied by any given moment and of the relative weight that each requires, then there can be no disagreement about the meaning(s) of any text written in that language. (Where several co-exist, they are to be harmoniously arranged in a determinate order, much as medieval exegesis, governed by a similar, if somewhat more explicit, set of principles and objectives, did with holy scripture.) Conflict over interpretations could then only arise from erroneous (or perverse) uses of language.

3. Derrida discusses this 'confrontation' in terms of 'two interpretations of interpretation, of structure, of sign, of play', in *Writing and Differences*, trans. Alan Bass (London, 1978), pp. 278–93, especially pp. 292–3. [Cf. Gabriele Schwab's reference to this idea of Derrida's, p. 98, n. 4. Ed.]

4. For the difference between 'closure' and 'end', see Derrida, *Writing and Difference*, p. 250.

5. See, for example, Schelling's discussion of the cleavage (*Spaltung*) between the subjective and the objective (the ideal and the real, speculation and empiricism) that resulted from (self-) reflection and that only an idealist philosophy of nature could overcome.

6. Cf. Martin Heidegger, *Identity and Difference*, trans. J. Stambaugh (New York, 1969), pp. 42–74.

7. See Dominic LaCapra, *Madame Bovary on Trial* (Ithaca, 1982), pp. 19–20, n. 2 for a discussion of the undecidable in the works of Derrida.

8. Cf. Friedrich Nietzsche, *Philosophy in the Tragic Age of the Greeks*, trans. M. Cowan (Chicago, 1962), p. 79.

9. For a discussion of Aristotle's formulation of identity, see Heidegger, *Identity and Difference*, pp. 24–6.

10. The first phrase is from the English version of the text, *Endgame, followed by Act Without Words* (New York, 1958), the second is my translation of the corresponding phrase from the French version, *Fin de partie* (Paris, 1957). References to these texts will be abbreviated hereafter to *E* and *FP* and incorporated parenthetically in my text. When the English version is significantly different from the French, I have provided my own translation.

11. For a discussion of the *sorites*, or heap paradox, from the perspective of modern analytical philosophy, see Max Black, *Margins of Precision* (Ithaca, NY, 1970), pp. 1–13: 'To argue that the *sorites* shows that something is wrong with logic would be like maintaining that the coalescence of raindrops reveals an imperfection in simple arithmetic' (p. 13).

12. Derrida refers to the problematic nature of the '*ça*' in *Limited Inc.*, supplement to *Glyph* (Baltimore, 1977) 2:81 n. 7 and in *Glas* (Paris, 1974).

13. Adorno, 'Towards an Understanding of *Endgame*', p. 113.

14. Heidegger, following Nietzsche, describes how in its more extreme forms, the scientific mentality shares with philosophical idealism a fundamental mistrust and even hatred of this world: see Martin Heidegger, *Basic Writings*, ed. D. F. Krell (New York, 1977), pp. 269–92.

15. Newton was profoundly interested in the apocalyptic books of the Bible – Daniel and Revelations – which he believed revealed the dominion of God over history as natural philosophy revealed His dominion over nature. See Richard S. Westfall, *Never a Rest: A Biography of Isaac Newton* (Cambridge, 1980), especially pp. 817–27.

16. Heinrich Heine, *Germany*, in *The Works of Heinrich Heine*, trans. C. G. Leland (New York, n.d.) vol. 9, pp. 142–4.

17. Hippolyte Taine, quoted in René Gibaudan, *Les idées sociales de Taine* (Paris, 1928), p. 158 (my translation).

18. Georg Lukács, *Realism in Our Time: Literature and the Class Struggle*, trans. John and Necke Mander (New York, 1964), p. 32.

19. Cavell, 'Ending the Waiting Game', p. 130.

20. See Beckett's *How It Is* (London, 1964), where the mud is a constant and cannot be eliminated.

21. See, for example, Beckett's *Catastrophe*, in *Complete Dramatic Works* (London, 1986), pp. 455–61.

22. Cf. Heidegger's discussion in *Basic Writings*, pp. 283–318, 369–92.

23. For an extended discussion of 'regulated play', see Derrida, *Writing and Difference*, pp. 278–94.

8

Adoption in 'Endgame'

PAUL LAWLEY

I

The terminal world of Beckett's *Endgame*, with its 'corpsed'[1] aspect outside the stage-refuge and its barbed play inside, sustains life solely, it seems, by reason of its ruler's procrastination. 'Enough, it's time it ended, in the refuge too', proclaims Hamm at the outset. 'And yet I hesitate, I hesitate to ... to end' (p. 93). His hesitation is a problem not least because of 'that hatred of nature as process (birth and copulation and death) which runs through the whole play'.[2] For if Hamm's hesitation necessitates a prolongation of life in the refuge, the processes of nature, in one form or another, are surely unavoidable.

There is one course of action open to Hamm which offers perpetuation of life without direct involvement in the processes of nature: adoption. Indeed, this seems to be a vital means of continuation for the (now) refuge-dynasty. The legless, ashbin-bound Nagg and Nell are the biological parents of Hamm, but Hamm's central narrative, referred to by him as his 'chronicle' (p. 121) though presented as a fiction, provides a possible version of the adoption of Clov, Hamm's present servant and 'son'.[3] The crucial question towards the end of the play surrounds the possible adoption of a small boy reported by Clov to be still alive outside the refuge. In view of these instances, one is not surprised that, according to S. E. Gontarski, a note written as Beckett was embarking on a two-act holograph of the play 'suggests that [Hamm's] father and son are adopted; that is, Nagg too may have been someone taken into the shelter as a servant: "A un père adoptif/un fils adoptif"'.[4] Thus

119

although three generations are represented on the stage, we cannot be sure, despite what is said, that the characters constitute a genetic line.

The connection between adoption and servanthood is an important one. Hamm sees all relationships, whether with his 'son' or with his toy dog (these two are associated more than once⁵), with his retainers or with his 'bottled' father, in terms of dominance and servitude. Upon an adopted son he can bring to bear a pressure of obligation:

> **Hamm** ... It was I was a father to you.
> **Clov** Yes. (*He looks at* **Hamm** *fixedly.*) You were that to me.
> **Hamm** My house a home for you.
> **Clov** Yes. (*He looks about him.*) This was that for me.
> **Hamm** (*Proudly.*) But for me (*gesture towards himself*) no father. But for Hamm (*gesture towards surroundings*) no home.
>
> (pp. 110–11)

The adopted child is expected to feel he owes a debt because he was *chosen*. The trouble with biological parenthood, as one of the play's funniest exchanges suggests, is that you can't choose:

> **Hamm** Scoundrel! Why did you engender me?
> **Nagg** I didn't know.
> **Hamm** What? What didn't you know?
> **Nagg** That it'd be you.
>
> (p. 116)

Hamm's experience in his relationship with Clov has been one of dominance and control, as much now (at least on the face of it) as in the scenario of choice so lovingly fictionalised in the chronicle. In contrast Nagg has always been a subject of his son. In his toothless second childhood, the immobile papa calls out to his own child for 'me pap!' (p. 96), and, having been tricked into listening to Hamm's chronicle by the promise of a non-existent sugar-plum, he presents a rich counterpoint to his current situation in his 'curse'. The counterpoint suggests that Hamm has retained power over his father not by growing into an independent adult but by remaining a dependent son:

> Whom did you call when you were a tiny boy, and were frightened, in the dark? Your mother? No. Me. We let you cry. Then we moved you out of earshot, so that we might sleep in peace. (*Pause.*) I was asleep, as happy as a king, and you woke me up to have me listen to you. It

wasn't indispensable, you didn't really need to have me listen to you.
Besides I didn't listen to you. (*Pause.*) I hope the day will come when
you'll really need to have me listen to you, and need to hear my voice,
any voice.

(p. 119)

Hamm's *need*, both then and now (despite Nagg's claim), is the need
to exert power wilfully, even arbitrarily. As a biological son yet an
adoptive father he is in an ideal position to fulfil that need.

Nagg's curse presents a scene of familial usurpation ('as happy as a
king') and in doing so invites an Oedipal interpretation. Yet *Endgame* is concerned less with the dynamics of relations between father
and mother and son than, as I have suggested, with the opposition of
two kinds of dynastic perpetuation, biological and adoptive. In the
following analysis I want to consider the significance of adoption,
first in Hamm's chronicle, then in the play as a whole.

II

Alternating its 'narrative tone' with the 'normal tone' used by Hamm
to comment on his own varying powers of composition, the chronicle
(pp. 116–18) tells of how a surviving vassal of Hamm's came
begging him for bread for his child. Hamm recounts how, though
doubting the very existence of the child, he proceeded to berate the
man for his stupidity, optimism and irresponsibility. The climax of
the narrative, Hamm's decision about the child, is prepared with
relish but never delivered:

> In the end he asked me would I consent to take in the child as well – if
> he were still alive. (*Pause.*) It was the moment I was waiting for.
> (*Pause.*) Would I consent to take in the child . . . (*Pause.*) I can see him
> still, down on his knees, his hands flat on the ground, glaring at me
> with his mad eyes, in defiance of my wishes. (*Pause. Normal tone.*) I'll
> soon have finished with this story. (*Pause.*) Unless I bring in other
> characters. (*Pause.*) But where would I find them? (*Pause.*) Where
> would I look for them? (*Pause. He whistles. Enter* **Clov.**) Let us pray
> to God.
>
> (p. 118)

The melodrama of the confrontation with the defiant vassal rather
distracts from the decision about adoption, but it enables an
effectively bathetic interruption to be made by the narrator's reflex-
ive anxieties. The contrast is jolting, yet there is a striking similarity

of phrasing which occurs across the division of 'narrative' and
'normal' tones: 'Would I consent to *take in* the child . . .'; 'Unless I
bring in other characters'.[6] The resemblance invites us to consider
the fictional*ised* situation in terms of the fictional*iser's* situation, the
narration of situation in terms of the situation of narration – and
vice-versa. The difference between the two dimensions is diminished
further by Hamm's speaking of the narrator's situation ('bring in
other characters') in spatial metaphors (*'where* would I *find*
them? . . . *Where* would I *look for* them?') which would apply
literally to the fictional situation (*where* was the vassal's child? –
'assuming he existed' [p. 117]). The aesthetic dimension of the
chronicle and the experiential dimension of the chronicler move into
identity through the figure of adoption: Hamm the tyrant might 'take
in the child' as Hamm the narrator might 'bring in other characters'.
In each case adoption is the sole means of continuance. We can go
further: in *Endgame* adoption is a figure for the fictional process
itself, the only acceptable means of self-perpetuation for characters
who reject the processes of nature.

A similar movement between dimensions is apparent when we
consider the idea of termination in the play. 'I'll soon have *finished
with* this story', says Hamm. When, moments later, Clov enters in
response to the whistle, he announces that there is a rat in the
kitchen:

> **Hamm**   And you haven't exterminated him?
> **Clov**   Half. You disturbed us.
> **Hamm**   He can't get away?
> **Clov**   No.
> **Hamm**   You'll *finish him* later. Let us pray to God.
>   (pp. 118–19, my emphasis)

To be finished *with* something is different from having finished it.
Yet the odd thing here is that though it is the narrator Hamm who
has finished *with* something, it is the rat-killer Clov whose activity is
spoken of in the way one might speak of a story: the story-teller
might be more frequently said to have *finished* his story than to have
finished *with* it. The aesthetic connotation of 'finish' (as opposed to
'finish with') is strongly present – largely because of insistent
repetition – in an earlier exchange:

> **Hamm**   Why don't you finish us? (*Pause.*) I'll tell you the combina-
> tion of the larder if you promise to finish me.

> **Clov** I couldn't finish you.
> **Hamm** Then you shan't finish me.
> (p. 110)

The primary meaning of 'finish' is clear. But, in addition, it is as though Hamm *himself* is a story that needs to be finished (off). The poise in (or of) the words is as delicate here as it is in the opening phrases of the play: 'Finished, it's finished, nearly finished, it must be nearly finished' (p. 93). Within Clov's sentence is the feeling not just of some experience coming to an end, but (especially after the opening ritual) of a predetermined pattern about to be completed. The inflections are distinct even though combined.[7]

The moment near the end of the play when Clov sights what looks 'like a small boy!' (p. 130) brings together the themes of adoption (and continuance through fiction) and of termination. Having made the sighting, Clov makes for the door with the gaff:

> **Hamm** No!
> (**Clov** *halts.*)
> **Clov** No? A potential procreator?
> **Hamm** If he exists he'll die there or he'll come here. And if he doesn't ...
> (*Pause.*)
> **Clov** You don't believe me? You think I'm inventing?
> (*Pause.*)
> **Hamm** It's the end, Clov, we've come to the end. I don't need you any more.
>
> (pp. 130–1)

In this episode the adoption-decision is transferred out of the narrative dimension of the chronicle into the dimension of the action itself. Again a migration is effected: the episode from the fictional narrative is 'adopted' by the actual dramatic world, or, more accurately, by Clov. But, crucially, the element of indeterminacy in the chronicle-version ('assuming he existed') has now assumed a pivotal position. Hamm's decision to end turns, it seems, not upon the decision to take in or not take in the small boy, but upon his belief that Clov is 'inventing'. At last Hamm too perceives adoption as the figure of fiction-as-continuance. Even though Clov intends to kill the boy, it is his *proposal* of the fiction that matters, his attempt to *bring* the boy *in* to their life-story. Hamm resists. 'Not an underplot, I trust' (p. 130), he exclaims when Clov first registers an outside presence. He puts himself in the position of a spectator at his own endgame. 'It's the end ... we've come to the end' – not just of the experience but of the game's aesthetic pattern too: the statement is poised between the participator's (or actor's) perception of termination and the spectatorial perception of it. It is this profoundly uneasy poise which ultimately thwarts the 'attempt to determine if *Endgame* imitates the act of dying or whether it imitates a game in which the players pretend to move towards death'.[8]

III

Few texts can be more explicitly structured upon binary oppositions than *Endgame*. 'Outside of here it's death' (p. 96) announces Hamm, and in doing so he loads the onstage/offstage, inside/outside opposition with a decisive weight of signification. Upon this fundamental prescription the play's other oppositions – past/present, land/sea, nature/non-nature, light/darkness – depend.[9] Some of the routines and jokes even underline the habit of polarisation.

> (*Enter* **Clov** *holding by one of its three legs a black toy dog.*)
> **Clov**   Your dogs are here.
> (*He hands the dog to* **Hamm** *who feels it, fondles it.*)
> **Hamm**   He's white, isn't he?
> **Clov**   Nearly.
> **Hamm**   What do you mean, nearly? Is he white or isn't he?
> **Clov**   He isn't.
>
> (p. 111)

And when Clov reports that the light outside is 'GRREY!', Hamm queries the information, eliciting the confirmation: '*Light black. From pole to pole*' (p. 107, my emphasis).

The ubiquitous patterns of opposition form an essential context for the operation of the figure of adoption. We have seen that adoption, as presented in the play, involves a negotiation between the distinct areas or terms of an opposition, a crossing of vital boundaries for the purposes of the perpetuation of life. Yet if adoption is the agency of perpetuation, it is also an operation which cannot avoid compromising the stability of the world it is designed to maintain. In examining the climax of Hamm's chronicle, we were able to identify two distinct dimensions: that of the *narrative*, in which the fictionalised Hamm decides whether or not to take the vassal's child into the refuge, and that of the *narrator*, the actual dimension of the drama, in which the Hamm we see on the stage decides whether or not to bring other characters into his story. Although each of these dimensions insists upon a sharp inside/outside opposition, with a definite boundary, they *themselves*, despite separation by a boundary apparently no less definite (that between inset story and dramatic action, narrative of situation and situation of narrative) are blurred together by the association of the child Hamm might 'take in' and the characters he might 'bring in'. For this is an association, a merging, of Hamm's art and his life. His life contains art, certainly, but we cannot be sure that the reverse is not also true: does art 'contain' his life? Is he (self-) invented, a story? ('. . . if you promise to *finish* me.')

It is at the moment Clov sights – or invents – the small boy outside the refuge that the fictional chronicle impinges most strongly upon the stage-world. The process by which action echoes – or has been pre-echoed by – fiction at this point brings the question of the ontological status of the stage-world to crisis-point – and both characters recognise this. Hamm's refusal constitutes a decision not to adopt a fresh fiction into the stage-world rather than a decision not to take in a child. Indeed, by acknowledging the possibility of fiction ('You think I'm inventing?') Hamm is uncovering the process which has enabled the game to continue. Now he can begin to renounce: 'It's the end, Clov, we've come to the end . . .' And yet this renunciation of fiction can be read, and played, as a grand theatrical gesture, a richly fictional moment. As ever in Beckett, it is the imagination-dead-imagine stalemate.

In a chapter entitled 'Marking and Merging Horizons' in his book *The Modern Stage and Other Worlds*, Austin E. Quigley suggests that 'the glass walls marking the borders of Mrs Alving's house in Ibsen's *Ghosts* become, in many ways, a summarising image of the solid but permeable horizons of the modern theatre. The solid penetrability of the glass wall gradually becomes an emblem of repeatedly asserted but repeatedly undermined divisions between inner and outer, good and bad, past and present, self and other, and so on.'[10] The refuge of *Endgame* reproduces Mrs Alving's house in a terminal phase. The divisions are more starkly asserted and the mergings correspondingly more radical, for the zone of action is now ontological and being itself is at stake. The figure of adoption is the agency through which this world of divisions is perpetuated, yet it also precipitates those mergings which compromise the divisions. In this way it simultaneously establishes and renders unstable the very ground upon which *Endgame* is played out. Adoption in *Endgame* makes, and unmakes, a world of difference.

From *Modern Drama*, 31 (1988), 529–35.

NOTES

[This essay is a good example of how a critic may put to work the insights and opportunities offered by contemporary theory without explicitly espousing any particular theoretical cause or making inordinate demands of the reader's patience or technical knowledge. From a careful and attentive reading of the irregular family relationships in *Endgame*, Lawley derives a model of legitimate and illegitimate parenthood; he then goes on to suggest that this model may also be used to think about the forms of narrative in the play, in which questions of truth and invention seem to correspond to natural and adopted lineage. This reading tactic, in which the metaphors used by and within a text are made to stand as allegories for that text's own processes of representation and narration, has parallels in the work of critics such as Paul de Man and Jacques Derrida and proves to be a highly suggestive and profitable method for exploring Beckett's work. Ed.]

1. Samuel Beckett, *The Complete Dramatic Works* (London, 1986), p. 106. *Endgame* is reprinted on pp. 89–134. All references, cited parenthetically in the text, are to this volume.

2. Ronald Gaskell, *Drama and Reality* (London, 1972), p. 149.

3. See their exchanges about the chronicle on pp. 121–2 for hints that this is the story of Clov's adoption. Hamm does refer once (on p. 126) to Clov as his son.

4. S. E. Gontarski, *The Intent of Undoing in Samuel Beckett's Dramatic Texts* (Bloomington, 1985), p. 52.

5. In his first solo (p. 93), Hamm mentions the dog where we might expect him to mention Clov, and Clov remarks later that he has been trying to 'be off' '[e]ver since I was whelped' (p. 98). The plural in Clov's announcement when he brings the dog to Hamm, '[y]our dogs are here' (p. 111 – the passage is quoted in section III below), seems to be a rueful acknowledgement of the kinship between his own lame self and the lame dog. Of both of them it might be said: 'He's not a real dog, he can't go' (p. 120). Hamm enjoys the association of human and dog. Just as he imagines his toy dog begging him in a human, standing posture, he imagines his vassal begging him in a dog-like posture, 'down on his knees, his hands flat on the ground' (p. 118 – the passage is quoted in section II below). There is also, of course, Nagg's dog-biscuit (p. 97);

not to mention Clov's flea laying/lying 'doggo': 'If he was laying we'd be bitched' (p. 108).

6. Beckett's original French version of the text, *Fin de partie*, has 'recueillir' for 'take in' (the child) and 'introduire' for 'bring in' (other characters). (See Samuel Beckett, *Fin de partie* [Paris, 1957], pp. 74–5.) There is no echo, but although my argument is less easy to conduct in *linguistic* terms, the French does not undermine my larger contention. My analysis proceeds on the principle that the English is an independent *version* of the play and not merely a translation of the French original.

7. This paragraph is indebted to Ruby Cohn's brief discussion of 'finish' as a 'polysemic refrain' in *Just Play: Beckett's Theater* (Princeton, 1980), p. 55.

8. Charles R. Lyons, *Samuel Beckett* (London, 1983), p. 55.

9. For a fuller discussion of the play's patterns of opposition, see my 'Symbolic Structure and Creative Obligation in *Endgame*', *Journal of Beckett Studies*, 5 (1979), 49–53.

10. Austin E. Quigley, *The Modern Stage and Other Worlds* (London, 1985), p. 34.

9

The Doubling of Presence in 'Waiting for Godot' and 'Endgame'

STEVEN CONNOR

Beckett's turn to the theatre has often been represented as the expression of a longing for an art of visibility and tangibility as a relief from the epistemological disintegrations of the Trilogy which Beckett described in his interview with Israel Schenker in 1956 – 'no "I", no "have", no "being", no nominative, no accusative, no verb. There's no way to go on.'[1] Michael Robinson, for example, sees the theatre as 'the only direction in which a development was possible', since the theatre 'promises a firmer reality than a subjective mono-logue written and read in isolation; perhaps on the stage the reality behind the words may be revealed by the action which often contradicts that literal meaning'.[2] Beckett himself has testified to the sense of relief that he gets from working in drama: 'For me, theatre is first of all a relaxation from the labour of the novel. You are working with a certain space and with people in this space.'[3]

Perhaps the most emphatic statement of this view of Beckett's turn to the theatre is that offered by Alain Robbe-Grillet. Writing early in Beckett's dramatic career, he stressed the sense of sheer *presence* which is given by Vladimir and Estragon, deprived as they apparently are of all the conventional dramatic supports of script, plot or properties. We see them, he says, 'alone on stage, standing up, futile, with no future or past, irremediably present'.[4] For Robbe-Grillet, Beckett's theatre embodies the Heideggerean apprehension of

128

Dasein, of primordial being-there: 'The human condition, Heidegger says, is *to be there*. Probably it is the theatre, more than any other mode of representing reality, which reproduces this situation most naturally. The dramatic character is on stage, that is his primary quality: he is *there*' (*TNN*, 119). As Bruce Morrissette observes, Robbe-Grillet also finds in *Waiting for Godot* an assertion of Sartrean freedom *en situation*. The very absence of programme or *a priori* principles is what guarantees this freedom. Vladimir and Estragon have nothing to repeat; everything is happening for the first and last time: 'They are *there*; they must explain themselves. But they do not seem to have a text prepared beforehand and scrupulously learned by heart, to support them. They must invent. They are free' (*TNN*, 126).[5]

Other writers have elaborated or modified this theme by stressing the self-reflexiveness of the plays which, instead of undermining the audience's sense of presence, seems to intensify it, by focusing attention on the actual forms of the performance. William Worthen argues that Beckett 'literalises' the plight of his characters in the visibly straitened conditions in which his actors are required to work, so that a piece like *Play* 'dramatises the essential dynamics of stage performance'.[6] Sidney Homan argues in a similar way for self-reflection as a guarantee of presence. The plays turn in on themselves, he argues, to join playwright, play and audience in a mutually mirroring autonomy. The plays therefore no longer require reference to a pre-existing world, or the addition of any commentary to elucidate meanings which are hidden or allegorically elsewhere; the plays are simply what they are, in an elementary performing present, without before or after, the action 'complete, pure, itself – and immediately experienced by the audience'.[7] Beckett's occasional remarks about his plays have encouraged this view of their 'extreme simplicity of dramatic situation',[8] and his intense jurisdiction over his plays embodies this sense of their almost physical simplicity of form. In his direction, Beckett is concerned not so much to control the meaning or interpretation of his plays as to control this physical form, in the details of light, sound, decor and pacing.

In many ways, this view of Beckett's turn to the theatre reproduces conventional views about theatre itself and its relation to the other arts. It is conventional, for instance, to oppose the living art of the theatre to the dead or abstract experience of private reading. If we merely imagine characters and events in written texts, it is often said, then in the theatre, and in other visual media, we 'actually see' those characters and events, 'actually hear' their voices. Of course, the dramatic text usually exists in a written as well as in a physical form, but this double existence often focuses claims about the drama's difference from other arts. While it is usual to see the dramatic performance as subsidiary or secondary to the written text – in that it must be 'faithful' to it, must repeat it accurately and efficiently – it is also quite common to find the hierarchy reversed with the performance of the play claimed as its real or primary condition. Here, it is the written text which is considered to be empty or incomplete, while the essence of the play is embodied in that perfect production which fuses text and performance, idea and utterance. This need not be imagined as a single or particular performance: in one of the subtlest formulations of this principle, Hans-Georg Gadamer suggests that the essential nature of a play is developed in its slow organic evolution through different forms. In Gadamer's formulation, the model of the text as absolute origin and the performance as variable and imperfect repetition is abandoned, for now reproducibility guarantees the permanence of the being of the play through multiple embodiments.[9]

Another influential formulation of the belief in the priority of the performed play is that of Antonin Artaud. What makes Artaud's writings particularly useful for examining Beckett's work and the critical constitution of it is not only the widely diffused influence of Artaud's ideas, but his particular stress upon and opposition to repetition as a model for theatre. Throughout his essays of the 1930s, Artaud argues for a non-repetitive theatre, one no longer slavishly obedient to the written texts which precede and control it. The Theatre of Cruelty projected by Artaud escapes the tyranny of the verbal altogether and speaks its own, intrinsically theatrical language of mime, gesture, dance, music, light, space and scene. Throughout the essays in *The Theatre and its Double*, Artaud insists on the physicality of the theatre, maintaining that 'the stage is a tangible, physical place that needs to be filled and ought to be allowed to speak its own concrete language'.[10] Once the drama rediscovers its own language, Artaud argues, 'we can repudiate theatre's superstition concerning the script and the author's autocracy. In this way also we will link up with popular, primal theatre sensed and experienced directly by the mind, without language's distortions and the pitfalls in speech and words' ('The Theatre of Cruelty: Second Manifesto', *TD*, 82–3). This escape from the script is an escape from the compulsion to repeat. The spectator of the drama will no longer be forced to try to read the performance back into its original script, since what he or she beholds will be both performance and text. Closing the gap between text and performance will also eradicate the hiatus between meaning and interpretation for the spectator: 'This involved gesticulation we see has a goal, an immediate goal, towards which it aims by effective means, and we are able to experience its direct effectiveness. The thought it aims at, the states of mind it attempts to create, the mystical discoveries it offers are motivated and reached without delay or periphrasis' ('On the Balinese Theatre', *TD*, 42).

Of course, there is much in Artaud's formulation that is very unlike Beckett's theatre. Where the self-sufficiency of means in Beckett's work is a function of restriction and indigence, the self-proclaiming autonomy of Artaud's Theatre of Cruelty is an enactment of its 'blind zest for life'. Nevertheless, there are times when Artaud's arguments suggest very strongly the features of Beckett's theatre – or those features which criticism of Beckett has found most congenial: 'We might say the subjects presented begin on stage. They have reached such a point of objective materialisation we could not imagine them, however much one might try, outside this compact panorama, the enclosed, confined world of the stage' (*TD*, 43).

If, in one sense, Beckett's theatre is aptly described as a theatre of presence, or, in Artaud's terms, a theatre freed from repetition, then there are also important ways in which his work seems to undermine not only the particular claims of individual critics, but the more general cultural claims upon which they often rest and from which they derive their authority. It is no accident that Beckett's international fame came first of all as a playwright and not as a novelist, for it has been the prevailing critical and cultural consensus about the theatre and its strengths and capacities which has allowed his work to be absorbed and rewritten as a humanist theatre of presence, a theatre which directly and powerfully embodies real and universal human predicaments. In various ways, and particularly in the intricate play of its different repetitions, Beckett's theatre makes this critical representation seem inadequate, and asks questions of common conceptions about the theatre as a whole.

THE DOUBLING OF PRESENCE

One can understand why Robbe-Grillet should have found his views about the theatre so amply demonstrated in *Waiting for Godot*. It is undeniable that the restriction of the play's plot, setting and dialogue focus attention on the sheer fact of being on stage in a way that had never before been experienced so unrelievedly in the theatre. But what Robbe-Grillet doesn't explore are the implications of the fact that, as Vivian Mercier puts it, this is a play in which nothing happens, *twice*, in which Vladimir and Estragon undergo the ordeal of their sheer presence on stage, *twice*.[11] It is a repetition that makes all the difference, for it demonstrates to us that the sense of absolute presence is itself dependent upon memory and anticipation. We may see Vladimir and Estragon with our own eyes, and see them nowhere else but on the stage which is their only home, but this seeing has to contend with the knowledge that they have actually left the stage, have been or imagine themselves to have been elsewhere. At the beginning of Act II, we only recognise their being-back-again, or even their still-being-there, because of our awareness of the break that has taken place between the acts. Indeed, the appearance and meeting is established for us at the beginning of both acts as a repetition: – 'Is that you again?', 'You again'.[12] This, combined with the fact that Vladimir and Estragon do not leave the stage at the end of each act, but seem mysteriously to have left it at some point between Acts I and II, makes their continuing 'presence' on the stage something other than simple or unbroken.

To reappear, to be on stage again, is in itself to allow the shadow of absence or non-being to fall across the fullness and simplicity of *Dasein*. It opens up the dual anxiety of living in time, an anxiety expressing itself in the two questions 'am I the same as I was yesterday' and 'will I be the same as I am today?' When Vladimir and Estragon meet, they have painfully to reconstruct the events of the previous day. As an audience we are in the same position as Vladimir and Estragon, certain or almost certain of what we can remember about the events of the previous act, though we cannot be certain that this is indeed the previous 'day' that Vladimir refers to. To reconstitute the day in memory and representation is to open up that gap between the original and its repetition which can never entirely be closed, either for the characters or for their audience; we can never be sure again of the simple factuality of the day and its events. What is more, the present moment will come to seem more and more dependent upon recapitulation in the future. So, when Vladimir sees the boy for the second time, he is concerned to make sure that he will indeed tell Godot that he has seen them. Despite the uncertainties of memory and recapitulation, it is not enough simply for Vladimir to be there: he must confirm this simple present tense by reference to an anticipated retrospect.

Once repetition has been set up in the play, it proves to be congenital. Once the second act is revealed to be a repetition or near-repetition of the first, then the first itself loses its self-sufficient repletion. If the second act encounter with the boy sends us back to the similar encounter in the first act, then we may remember that this has already struck Vladimir as a repetition:

> Vladimir I've seen you before haven't I?
> Boy I don't know, sir.
> Vladimir You don't know me?
> Boy No, sir.
> Vladimir It wasn't you came yesterday?
> Boy No, sir.
> Vladimir This is your first time?
> Boy Yes, sir.
> *Silence.*
>
> (CDW, 47–8)

In a similar way, every presence in *Waiting for Godot* seems likely to turn out to be a ghostly repetition, or even an anticipation. (In the curious *déjà vu* structure of *Waiting for Godot*, it might even be possible to read the boy in the first act as a repetition-in-advance of the boy who appears at the end.) Stranded as they are in their agonising space of waiting, Vladimir and Estragon seem to encounter the paradox of all time; that is, that the only tense we feel has real verifiable existence, the present, the here-and-now, is in fact never here-and-now. The present tense can never simply 'be', because the 'now' of the present tense can only be apprehended the split-second before it happens, or the split-second after. It is never itself, but always the representation of itself, anticipated or remembered, which is to say, non-present. Vladimir and Estragon, stranded in the not-yet or intermission of waiting, poised between the past that they no longer inhabit and the future which cannot commence until the arrival of Godot, can never *be* fully in their present either. The longer they spend on the stage, the more, for them and for the audience, the simple immediacy of the present becomes drawn into the complex web of relationship and repetition that is all experience of time.

In fact, there seem to be two main versions of the repetitive enacted in *Waiting for Godot*. The first is circular, and suggests the impossibility of any stable present because past and future are ranged about it so ambiguously. The model for this kind of repetition is provided by the circular song which Vladimir sings at the beginning of Act II. In this, priority and progression seem to be disallowed, since every element in the song is both before and after every other element. The other model of repetition is linear. Some of the repetitions in *Waiting for Godot* seem to indicate not endless reduplication, but entropic decline. Chief among these is the re-appearance of Pozzo in Act II, blind and without his watch, with a servant who is now unable to think because dumb. In later plays, Beckett insists more and more on this kind of repetition-with-decrease, to give us, for example, the gradual burying of Winnie in the earth, the slowing down of the speakers in *Play*, the weakening of the auditor's gesture in *Not I* and the enfeebling of the woman's voice in *Rockaby*.

All these suggest repetitive series rather than repetitive circles. It is hard to say whether this kind of repetition is more or less corrosive of the audience's sense of presence. It would seem to be true that the idea of a repetitive series at least retains the direction of time, and therefore stabilises the repetition, for in a repetitive series it is possible to distinguish and rank different stages of decline, and consequently possible to mark the passage of time by them. This kind of repetitive series also seems to promise an end point which circular repetition does not.

But even in a repetitive series there is a decentring effect which makes the sense of immediate presence difficult to sustain. For how do we begin to consider the two 'halves' of a Beckett da capo play? As with all such repetitions the first time through will strike us as new, and primary, and the second is likely to seem a derivation from the first, its ghost, or shadow. But the ubiquity of repetition and the insistence of series in Beckett's work prevents us from seeing the first time through as necessarily primary, or the second time through as terminal. Both are equally repetitions, and we are therefore deprived of the sense of priority or finality; each is doubled on the inside, as it were, by what it repeats, and what will repeat it. This is surely the reason why Beckett's repetitive structures rarely go into a third phase (though the Trilogy might seem to be an important exception). To pass into a third phase is to risk suggesting transcendence, or committing oneself at least to the triangular shape of transcendence as it has been conceived in many philosophical models; it is to rank the previous two possibilities as opposites and perhaps to suggest their dialectic subsuming or resolution in the third repetition. Here, repetition is the sign of redemption, the guarantee of memory and destiny. It might also be to remind one, in a less exalted way, of the superstitious values attached to the third repetition in myth and fairy tale, which always marks the moment of return, or the resolution into pattern of endless open process. The fixity conventionally established by the triad is most plainly stated by Lewis Carroll's Bellman, in *The Hunting of the Snark*, when he declares 'what I tell you three times is true'.[13] Beckett's theatre, on the other hand, leaves repetitive possibilities to extend arbitrarily and uncontrollably into the future beyond the play – and therefore in a sense to infiltrate the performance too.

One exception to this prevailing double-structure might seem to be *Endgame* – and this is also the most uncompromising representation in Beckett's work of repetition allied to entropic running down. Certainly, Hamm and Clov may be on the point of leaving at the end. But it might still be argued that withholding the repetition of the day from the audience has the effect of highlighting the self-sufficiency, the unique presence of this particular passage of time in a way that distinguishes it from other plays. We know that these players will return to the stage night after night – but, in the theatre, we see them once and for all.

Another way of putting this might be to say that *Endgame* impresses us with its unity. It is a unity which is foregrounded by repetitive devices. Beckett said of the play that it 'is full of echoes, everything answers itself',[14] and there does indeed seem to be a thickening of internal repetition in the play. The various parallels in the action, Clov watching Hamm at the beginning and the end of the play, Hamm taking off and putting on his old handkerchief, and the verbal echoes in Hamm's first and last soliloquies, as well as the repetitions of words and phrases shared by Hamm and Clov, all seem to give a sense of closure, completeness and self-identity to *Endgame*.[15]

But against all this are the various factors which resist this apprehension of unity. Near the beginning of the play, Hamm asks Clov 'What's happening, what's happening?', only to receive the reply 'Something is taking its course' (*CDW*, 98). These words suggest the non-identity of experience and meaning. If all that is happening is precisely what we see, consists simply in the two characters being there, then, for Hamm and Clov, this being there is agonisingly insufficient. For Hamm especially, meaning or significance cannot inhere in experience, but must be imposed from the outside, as the supervention of an imagined outsider, a 'rational being' who, as he surmises, might happen to visit them and 'get ideas into his head' (*CDW*, 108). Because of this dependence on meanings ascribed from the outside, the endless process of Hamm's and Clov's lives never comes of itself to any point of significance or understanding; the best that can be managed is the asymptotic approach to meaning or identity which is imaged in the allusions to the millet-heap of the philosopher Sextus Empiricus. Clov looks forward to the coming of being as one looks for the moment when a succession of millet-grains added one to another can suddenly be recognised as a heap: 'Grain upon grain, one by one, and one day, suddenly, there's a heap, a little heap, the impossible heap' (*CDW*, 93). When the metaphor recurs in Hamm's words, it seems clear that the moment when the grain becomes a heap will recede infinitely: 'Moment upon moment, pattering down, like the millet grains of . . . (*he hesitates*) . . . that old Greek, and all life long you wait for that to mount up to a life' (*CDW*, 126). In this hell, as in Sartre's *Huis Clos*, it proves impossible to imagine a life brought to completeness. When death comes it will not confer a meaning, but will simply, arbitrarily, bring the process of living to a halt.[16]

So we can see that *Endgame* refuses the consummation of an ending which its form and title suggest. Time and again in Beckett's work, we encounter the anxiety that it will not be possible to come to an end because there will have been no full existence prior to that ending; and, for all its powerful theatrical presence, *Endgame* shows us characters who fear that they will never have been enough in the present to vanish. Hamm shares with characters in the Trilogy, especially the voice in *The Unnamable*, that repetitive structure of consciousness, in which it is impossible to be fully oneself, because fullness of being is always one step further on, always deferred to the future. Hamm's life, as he says, was always 'the life to come' (*CDW*, 116). As Robbe-Grillet recognises, a present contaminated in this way by lack ceases to exist: 'under these conditions, the present becomes nothing, it disappears, it too has been conjured away, and lost in the general bankruptcy' (*TNN*, 129).

If Hamm's life is always deferred, then it is also true that it is a life lived in repetition and retrospect. It is as though every unfinished moment requires repetition to bring it to completeness, or significance. So, as we listen to his endless attempts to retrieve the past in his portentous narrative we sense what may happen to the present moment. As in *Waiting for Godot*, the present fades into its reconstitution in future repetition. Indeed, for all the locked closure of this play, there is an insistent self-doubling that takes place at every moment. This, surely, is the effect of all the moments of theatrical self-reflexiveness in the play, Hamm's posturing grandiloquence, mimicked by Nagg's story, Clov's sarcasm at the audience's expense and the references to 'playing' of all kinds, from Hamm's opening words to the explicit references to asides, exits and soliloquies. All these features induce consciousness not of the stage as simply itself, but of the stage as a space of representation – even if it is the minimal representation of itself. No matter what is stripped away of character, plot and setting on the stage, there always persists, within the most reduced performance, a residual self-doubling – the stage representing itself *as* stage, *as* performance. If we see *Endgame* initially as a play which acts out the coming to an end of one kind of repetitive series, then in another clear sense it is a play which demonstrates the necessary and inescapable continuation of repetition. This necessity is described well by Jacques Derrida in his critique of Artaud's prescriptions for the Theatre of Cruelty:

> There is no theatre in the world today which fulfils Artaud's desire. And there would be no exception to be made for the attempts made by Artaud himself. He knew this better than any other: the 'grammar' of the theatre of cruelty, of which he said that it is 'to be found', will always remain the inaccessible limit of a representation which is not repetition, of a *re*-presentation which is full presence, which does not carry its double within itself as its death, of a present which does not repeat itself, that is, of a present outside time, a non-present. The present offers itself as such, appears, presents itself, opens the stage of time or the time of the stage only by harbouring its own intestine difference, and only in the interior fold of its original repetition, in representation.[17]

The moment of pure theatre which Beckett seems to show us, Hamm declaiming as an actor in the dying moments of the play, with no pretence that he is anything else, is in reality not the limit of full self-identity. The actor who plays the part of Hamm cannot – by definition – be the same actor whose part Hamm represents himself as playing. There is certainly close resemblance between the two, but if we recognise the collusion between the actor who speaks the words of the text and the character who repeats the words of his oft-rehearsed story, then that is because we also recognise the sustaining difference between them. In other words, we recognise the resemblance as one of repetition rather than identity. And the closer the performance comes to an identity with its text, the more Derrida's obstinate 'interior fold of its original repetition' reasserts itself.

There is another way of thinking about this. For the theatre to be theatre, it must be observed, must be staged in a particular place for a particular audience. Traditionally, the playwright and actor have depended upon, and sometimes regretted, this necessity. Billie White-law has recently said that Beckett himself thinks of his plays as ideally a drama without an audience. But, though it is certainly possible to imagine a performance without an audience, it is doubtful whether such a thing could count for anyone as a performance unless the element of spectacle were retained. This residual doubling asserts itself at the moment of Hamm's withdrawal from the theatre at the end of the play. After he has discarded all his petty theatrical paraphernalia, he is left merely with words and, when they cease, with darkness and silence. His final words seem to show him embracing this final retreat. His story has concerned his rebuff to the man he has hired (Clov?), whose son he would not permit to live with them. But if Clov is a kind of son to Hamm, then the closure of possibility in Hamm's story is contradicted by Clov's continuing presence on stage. Hamm's words may seem like an embracing of solitude, but they show in their hesitations and gaps the awareness of a potential audience – for example in the phrase 'there we are, there I am, that's enough', in which the second phrase sounds like a retraction or correction of the first. However, the first person plural recurs a little later when, having whistled and sniffed to see if Clov is still alive and then having cautiously called his name, he settles back, saying 'Good . . . Since that's the way we're playing it . . . let's play it that way . . . and speak no more about it' (*CDW*, 133). The conventional 'we' here includes the possibility that Clov may still be there, as indeed he is, and may help to confirm the audience's suspicion that this little scene has been played out between them before. The last lines of the play have Hamm withdrawing into solitude, after he has pierced the barrier between audience and spectacle with the whistle that he throws into the auditorium. But Hamm's solitude remains an enacted solitude, enacted for us and for the still-visible Clov. Hamm has discarded all but his 'old stancher', and closes his soliloquy with an affectionate address to it – 'You . . . remain' (*CDW*, 134). The irresistible affect of his words is to suggest the presence of the audience who do indeed remain, for the time being anyway, watching him. Hamm's words seem to acknowledge the necessity of the Other, even as he repudi-ates it. Only as long as they 'remain' to watch can he 'remain' in enacted solitude.

From Steven Connor, *Samuel Beckett: Repetition, Theory and Text* (Oxford, 1988), pp. 115–25.

NOTES

[This essay is taken from my own book on Beckett. This attempts to account for the obvious and emphatic force of repetition in Beckett's work in the light of the poststructuralist accounts of repetition to be found in the work of the French theorists Gilles Deleuze and Jacques Derrida. Both of these argue that repetition is highly ambivalent in the Western philosophical tradition. Repetition confirms the priority of ideas of original truth and presence over the idea of the copy or the derivation, but it also puts that structure at risk, by suggesting that an otherwise free-standing truth or absolute is in some uncanny way dependent upon the copy that repeats it (the original version of a text might then be thought of as dependent upon a translated version of itself, or a playscript upon its performance). The insistence of repetition in Beckett's work, and especially in *Waiting for Godot* and *Endgame* therefore puts into question many of our assumptions about truth, reality and presence, and especially our assumptions about the immediacy and reality of the theatrical experience. Ed.]

1. 'Moody Man of Letters', *New York Times*, Sunday May 6 1956, section 2, p. 3.

2. Michael Robinson, *The Long Sonata of the Dead: A Study of Samuel Beckett* (New York, 1969), p. 230.

3. Quoted in *Materialen zu Becketts 'Endspiel'*, ed. Michael Haerdter (Frankfurt, 1968), p. 88 (my translation).

4. 'Samuel Beckett, or Presence on the Stage', in *Snapshots and Towards a New Novel* (London, 1965), p. 119. References hereafter abbreviated to *TNN* and incorporated in the text.

5. See the discussion in Bruce Morrissette, 'Robbe-Grillet as a Critic of Samuel Beckett', in *Samuel Beckett Now: New Critical Approaches to the Novels, Poetry and Plays*, 2nd edn, ed. Melvin J. Friedman (Chicago and London, 1975), pp. 59–72.

6. 'Beckett's Actor', *Modern Drama*, 26 (1983), 420.

7. Sidney Homan, *Beckett's Theaters: Interpretations for Performance* (London and Toronto, 1984), p. 49.

8. Beckett, in a letter to Alan Schneider, 29 December 1957, in *Disjecta: Miscellaneous Writings and A Dramatic Fragment*, ed. Ruby Cohn (London, 1983), p. 109.

9. See the discussion of drama and art in general as historical 'play' in Hans-Georg Gadamer, *Truth and Method* (London, 1981), pp. 104–7.

Joel Weinsheimer summarises Gadamer's views on the relationship of play-text and performance in the following terms in his *Gadamer's Hermeneutics: A Reading of 'Truth and Method'* (New Haven and London, 1985), pp. 109–10:

> When something is imitated, when it is represented and recognised as something (else), it becomes something more than what it was, and that 'more' is that it becomes itself more fully. Gadamer suggests that the same happens when anything is transformed into a Gebilde – that is, when it becomes repeatable by being repeated (other-wise) in an artwork. Performance is not something ancillary, accidental, or superfluous that can be distinguished from the play proper. The play proper exists first and only when it is played. Performance brings the play into existence and the playing of the play is the play itself . . . Thus, the work cannot be differentiated from the representations of it since it exists only *there*, only in the flesh. It comes to be in representation and in all the contingency and particularity of the occasions of its appearance.

10. 'Production and Metaphysics', in *The Theatre and Its Double*, trans. Victor Corti (London, 1970), p. 27. References hereafter are abbreviated to *TD* and incorporated in the text.

11. Vivian Mercier, 'The Uneventful Event', *Irish Times*, 18 February 1956, p. 6.

12. *Waiting for Godot*, in *Samuel Beckett: The Complete Dramatic Works* (London, 1986), pp. 10, 53. References both to *Waiting for Godot* and *Endgame* will be to this edition, abbreviated hereafter to *CDW* and incorporated parenthetically in the text.

13. *The Complete Works of Lewis Carroll* (London, 1939), p. 680.

14. Quoted in Haerdter, *Materialen zu Becketts 'Endspiel'*, p. 46 (my translation).

15. A full account of these verbal repetitions in *Endgame* can be found in Ruby Cohn's *Just Play: Beckett's Theater* (Princeton, 1980), pp. 107–15.

16. There has been some dispute about the origin of the millet-grain metaphor. Some writers have identified it with Zeno's heap of grain which is endlessly divisible in two, though it is hard to see the application of this to the situation in *Endgame*. Hugh Kenner's attribution of the metaphor to the philosopher Sextus Empiricus seems the most satisfactory (*A Reader's Guide to Samuel Beckett* [London, 1973], p. 123). It is confirmed by Alice and Kenneth Hamilton in *Condemned to Life: The World of Samuel Beckett* (Grand Rapids, 1976), p. 220.

17. 'The Theater of Cruelty or the Closure of Representation', in *Writing and Difference*, trans. Alan Bass (London, 1978), p. 248.

10

A Blink in the Mirror: Oedipus and Narcissus in 'Waiting for Godot' and 'Endgame'

JUDITH A. ROOF

Referring to Clov's inability to sit and his own inability to stand, Hamm proudly but paradoxically states in Samuel Beckett's *Endgame*, 'Every man his speciality'.[1] The daily struggle of 'I can't go on, I'll go on', a struggle against specialisation or lack that represents a loss of physical facility through time, takes its course through the history of Hamm's narratives and Nell's memory in *Endgame*, through Winnie's stories in *Happy Days*, and through Vladimir's and Estragon's dim memories of youth in *Waiting for Godot*. Each character in the pairs of characters has indeed become specialised through history. In each play the characters' former wholeness, the subject of renewed reverie and thwarted recovery, is translated into the characters' present limitations – Hamm's blindness, Clov's inability to sit, Winnie's entrapment in the mound, Vladimir's bladder problems, and Estragon's problems with his feet. In short, specialisation is the result of an historical evolution of lack. The limitations are the recognised result of the passage of time; and thus the recounting of history is the tracing of the image of a formerly total self, while the loss of wholeness through time is poignantly apparent in the image of the other character in the pair who has lost as well, but who retains precisely that which has been lost on the part of the other character. Each character in a pair opposes the other, providing the mirror image not of what is present but of what is no longer present in each.

The mirroring which informs the relationships of the characters in the pairs is a mirror image in so far as it is a reversal, a literal opposition, and in so far as the characters take their cues from the lack(s) evident in the other character. The suggestion of the mirroring of characters in these plays is the suggestion of a narcissism grown sour, of a deadly entrapment of the gaze in a now-stagnant pool. However, what appears to be a narcissistic structure is not; the dynamic between these paired characters is not so much one of an opposition or of an irresistible attraction, but of a filling in, of a supplementariness, a 'specialisation', which forces the constant redefinition of self in terms of the past and in terms of the other. The pairs interact in a dialectical dynamic, from present to past, from one to the other, in an alternation which is ultimately an evocation of an oedipal search for identity through the morass of an endless history.

Genuine narcissism, in the form of a libidinous investment in the mind's own eye, appears paradoxically to emerge when Beckett changes from pairs of characters to triangles in *Play* (1963), in *Come and Go* (1968), and later in *Catastrophe* (1982). Abandoning pairs, Beckett peoples these plays with triads – M, W1 and W2 in *Play*, Flo, V and Ru in *Come and Go*, and the Director, Assistant Director and Protagonist in *Catastrophe*. What appears to be the suggestion of an oedipal triangle in these plays shifts from a completely oedipal revision of the past in *Play* and *Come and Go* or of the stage in *Catastrophe* to a narcissistic gaze into self within the oedipal which reflects the opposition and specularity of the relationship between the audience and the stage. The shift from the oedipal to a narcissism enabled by the oedipal in the corpus of Beckett's drama is an alternation which not only moves from dyads to triads in individual plays, but which works within the plays themselves as an alternation between the oedipal search for identity and the deadly rest of the narcissistic gaze. In this context, moving from the oedipal to the narcissistic is not a regression, nor is the subsequent return to the oedipal stage a maturation; the drama is simply an alternation from one to the other, analogous to the alternation from A to B to A in *Act Without Words II*.

What is oedipal and what is narcissistic in Beckett's drama is defined by the characters' ability to perceive the totality of them-

selves in their images reflected in the other as well as by their ability
to keep such recollection within the spectacle, within language, and
within their interaction with other characters. Not a question of plot
or conflict, the oedipal refers primarily to the question of one's
identity and relation to others as that devolves on stage. In relation to
this mirror of the stage and the mirrored characters, the oedipal is the
expression of the symbolic perception of totality which is inaugur-
ated by the stage in development Lacan names the 'Mirror Stage'.
The narcissistic is, then, the gaze at self in the mirror, an act only
understood after a perception of totality, in other words, historically.
In this way the oedipal enables a perception of the narcissistic which
precedes it chronologically.

In 'The Mirror Stage' Lacan calls the episode of the child gazing at
his/her image in the mirror 'a drama'.[2] For Lacan the mirror stage is
the point at which the child, still immobile, recognises via the total
image of him or herself in the mirror the idea of a totality of body
and self not yet acquired. As Lacan states:

> The mirror stage is a drama whose internal thrust is precipitated from
> insufficiency to anticipation – and which manufactures for the subject,
> caught up in the lure of spatial identification, the succession of
> fantasies that extends from a fragmented body-image to a form of its
> totality that I shall call orthopaedic – and, lastly, to the assumption of
> the armour of an alienating identity, which will mark with its rigid
> structure the subject's entire mental development.[3]

As a drama, the process described by Lacan proceeds from 'insufficiency to anticipation', from 'the image of the body in bits and
pieces' to an image of totality. At the same time, the process proceeds
in the opposite direction toward a retroactive recognition of a past
fragmentation which is comprehended only once the child perceives
the image as total. The mirror stage thus appears to be the opposite
of the history of Beckett's characters, who in a present fragmented
state remember a totality.

The impetus of the mirror stage, then, is the action of recognising
both the wholeness of the image projected into the mirror and the
fragmentation from which one has just escaped: it is a drama of a
placement within history, through which both knowledge and wholeness become relative. The drama is a point of transition from
timelessness into time, from present to future to a recognition of past
as past made by means of visual perception. As Lacan later writes:
'What realises itself in my history, is not the past definite of what was

since it is no longer, nor even the present perfect of what has been in what I am, but the future anterior of what I will have been for what I am in the process of becoming.'[4] Because what is perceived, like a drama, is an illusion, the mirror stage is always a misperception, a misrecognition which nonetheless leads to a greater understanding and a greater terror. The mirror stage is the tragedy of perpetual loss, of the acquisition of a rigid 'armour', of an entry into the anxiety of history as well as a moment of jubilation and 'self-mastery'.

The illusion of unity the child perceives in the mirror, in which a human being is always looking forward to self-mastery, entails a constant danger of sliding back again into the chaos from which he or she started. 'It hangs over the abyss of a dizzy Ascent in which one can perhaps see the very essence of anxiety.'[5] This anxiety is comparative, the result of seeing a past during which self-mastery was missing, but it is also the foundation of an oedipal question of relation and identity. The mirror stage is 'an identification' with an image of totality, a moment which commences the child's relation to the image in the mirror as an image of an other, a relation which enables the oedipus complex.

While thrusting the child into a kind of knowledge which forces him or her into an oedipal search for identity and relation to others, the mirror stage also enables narcissism, since the image of self is first comprehended at the mirror stage.[6] This 'primary narcissism' is in dynamic opposition with the sexual libidinous investment represented by the oedipal conflict. The libidinal investment in self at the moment of the mirror stage, while making possible the oedipal, also provides the tension between the two libidos, tension Lacan connects to the 'existential negativity' grasped 'only within the limits of self-sufficiency of consciousness'.[7] In drama, as in the mirror stage, the oedipal comprehends both an oedipal, sexual libido and a narcissistic libido. The difference between them lies in the direction of the gaze of the character: in the oedipal the gaze is directed toward another person, place or time; in the narcissistic, the character's gaze is directed to or returned to self.

The connections among the drama of the mirror stage, the oedipus complex, and the notion of the centrality of an oedipal search for identity in theatre as suggested by Francis Fergusson and André Green is the relationship among the ability to perceive totality acquired at the mirror stage (the initial ability to form and relate to an image and an access to the symbolic), the specific content of the later Oedipus complex, and the repetition and reflection in theatre of both this ability to identify and an oedipal content open to the gaze of the audience. Fergusson makes the connection between theatre and the story of Oedipus: '*Oedipus Rex* is a crucial instance of drama, if not *the* play which best exemplifies this art in its essential nature and completeness.'[8] *Oedipus Rex* is an instance of the question of an identity dependent upon the unravelling of history and a gradual enlightenment open to the gaze of the audience. Like the mirror stage, the perception of the image, or of identity, changes the act of perception forever. 'The object, indeed, the final perception, the "truth", looks so different at the end from what it did at the beginning that Oedipus's action itself may seem not a quest, but its opposite, a flight.'[9] Like a child at the mirror stage, Oedipus moves toward a mastery of self at the same time that he apprehends the horror of a chaos which underlies that mastery.

The structure of the drama itself is reliant upon the tensions of the mirror stage. Like the mirror stage, 'the theatre has its effect only in so far as its ways are misunderstood by the spectators'.[10] What is thought to be seen on stage is not what is seen; it is mis-taken. The watching of a play, like the gaze into the mirror 'seems to drive the action outside of itself' by the very fact of the gaze or participation in the image.[11] A 'recognition by representation', theatre, like the mirror stage, proceeds from an 'ignorance to knowledge – whether on the part of the hero or the spectator'.[12] This (mis)recognition of what appears to be other, outside, as alienated is a resituation vis-à-vis the other in the image and in relation to what was that is no longer and what is that will soon no longer be.

In the work of Samuel Beckett, the relationship of the characters to the recognition mentioned by both Fergusson and Green seems to be reversed. Wholeness is retroactive and historical instead of fragmentation. The characters perceive their fragmentation in relation to a past wholeness instead of perceiving a past fragmentation in a present image of totality. Hamm posits an ironically positive proof that there is nature: 'But we breathe, we change! We lose our hair, our teeth! Our bloom! Our ideals!' (p. 11). As they are drawn back again and again to the question of former wholeness, Clov exclaims, 'We too were bonny – once. It's a rare thing not to have been bonny– once' (p. 42).

The dyadic plays, if a term may be coined for those plays in which pairs of characters interact as opposites, represent a primarily oedipal struggle in terms of history and the Other, centred around an anxiety about fragmentation and placement in history. The struggle to make time pass, to make waiting go more quickly, to fill up time is a struggle to regain the mastery and jubilation of the first glance in the mirror. Mastery for each character is always a memory recaptured fleetingly through Hamm's chronicles, Nagg's jokes, Winnie's stories, and Lucky's lecture. Jubilation, while sometimes past as in Nell's memories of Lake Como, is also projected into the future as a kind of grim jubilation when Godot comes, or night falls, or Winnie can play her music, or when Clov evokes his dream of a 'world where all would be silent and still and each thing in its last place, under the last dust' (p. 57).

The struggle to determine placement in space and time and identity in relation to one another is an oedipal struggle which takes place entirely in terms of the other character(s). Though there is some specifically oedipal content in Hamm's battles with his 'accursed progenitor' Nagg, or Vladimir's and Estragon's expectations from the ever-potential Godot, and in Winnie's relationship to Willie, the oedipal mode of these plays is a search for a placement in a history perpetually out of control, as evidenced by the constant lack in self as reflected in the presence in/of the other character. The mirrored characters reflect one another by responding to and by reassuring one another that they are no longer what they were and not yet what they are to be. Vladimir and Estragon fear to leave one another, yet constantly toy with the idea of parting, as do Hamm and Clov. Winnie fears that Willie will not appear from his hole. They remember each other's past, when Winnie wasn't trapped, when they were young on bicycles in the Ardennes, when there was plenty, when there was love.

The struggle to revise, refine the reality of a former illusion of totality in terms of the mirror Other is the impossibility that compels the visions of darkness and emptiness that stand as tempting mirages of peace when all time, and hence all history and struggle, cease. Thus, the ending of a 'day', of each long gaze, is crucial. In *Waiting for Godot* Vladimir and Estragon are left standing as night falls. Though they express a desire to go, they do not move. Though they indicate at the beginning of the second act that they have spent the night apart, night is no time of peace or relief. Estragon is beaten and Vladimir struggles with his bladder. Their static search for Godot is either unrelieved by the break in the gaze afforded by darkness, or darkness cannot finally loose them from the image of chaos that awaits each moment if Godot does not come. Although Hamm's blindness does not represent the insight of Oedipus, neither does not-seeing disable the function of the mirror. Darkness is no answer and Vladimir and Estragon are doomed to repeat, almost, the ritual of the daily mirror.

In *Endgame*, Clov's ending gaze at Hamm, who has escaped behind the veil of the stancher, is no escape or ending either. The gaze in the play is always Clov's – he is the locator in space. Hamm's blindness is the presence of vision in Clov, which Clov can see in its reflection as lack in Hamm. The final image of the play is not the vision of empty peace of which Clov has dreamed; rather, it is prototypical of the continuing mirror relationship of Hamm and Clov, with Clov surveying his own desire to escape in Hamm's unconsciousness – an unconsciousness which nonetheless provokes dreams that remind them both of their own missing parts and of amputation of the world. . . .

Though the characters in these earlier dyadic plays mirror one another and see themselves in one another in a way similar to the image the child sees in the mirror in the mirror stage, the characters are not fixed on an image of themselves in any kind of narcissistic gaze. They are fixed, rather, on the lack in self reflected by the other, since there is no escape from history or from each other in any of the plays. Paradoxically, the triadic plays, those with three central characters, superficially seem to be oedipal struggles as well; however, the characters in each of these plays appear to find a false resolution in narcissism, a narcissism which becomes merely a part of the overarching alternation between the oedipal and the narcissistic within the oedipal.

The first gaze of the mirror stage founds narcissism as well as the oedipal conflict. As Freud says in his essay 'On Narcissism: An Introduction', narcissism is a self-criticism of conscience based on self-observation. Seeking themselves as love objects, the narcissistic characters engage in a kind of self-preservative activity which leads the gaze inside to self instead of outside to the world. Narcissism is, thus, 'the libidinal complement to the egoism of the instinct of self-preservation'.[13] As the other half of the dialectic observed by Lacan between a narcissistic investment in an image of self and the oedipal sexual investment in the image of the Other, the narcissistic gaze appears to stop history, to stop time, and to prevent questions of placement and the anxiety of falling back into chaos. Narcissism is, however, also a paralysing illusion of joinder with self as Other rather than a jubilant image of totality. . . .

Watching theatre is gazing into the mirror, placing oneself between history and chaos. The alternation between oedipal and narcissistic is the essence of this mirror that enables and relies upon both. That Beckett's drama alternates this dynamic both within individual plays and within his work as a whole replicates this essential relationship between self and theatre, between audience and stage, between self and history, and between the experience of the audience and the search for identity afforded by the theatre. Like Oedipus, we are thrust into a history whence come both chaos and identity; like Narcissus, we gaze at the deadly pool whose only answers can be our own.

From *Myth and Ritual in the Plays of Samuel Beckett*, ed. Katherine H. Burkman (Rutherford, 1987), pp. 151–7, 162.

NOTES

[Judith A. Roof's essay, under the title 'A Blink in the Mirror: From Oedipus to Narcissus and Back in the Drama of Samuel Beckett', originally appeared in a volume of essays devoted to the importance of myth and ritual in Beckett's work; this shortened version misses out her discussion of plays other than *Waiting For Godot* and *Endgame*. The essay is included here as an example of the distinctive demands and rewards of an approach to Beckett informed by the psychoanalytic theory of Jacques Lacan. For Lacan, as for Beckett, the formation of the self takes place, not prior to, but through the operations of language, and the drama of the individual self is always a drama that involves the 'other'. This is only the first section of an essay that compares Beckett's early dramatic work, in which two-way or narcissistic relationships predominate, to later plays in which three-way, or 'oedipal' relationships are to the fore. But the burden of Roof's argument is that, whether in the narcissistic relationships of the mirror-stage, or the oedipal relationships of later psychological life, the self can never hope to know itself in its fullness or completeness. Beckett's work powerfully dramatises this painful failure to coincide with oneself. Ed.]

1. Samuel Beckett, *Endgame* (New York, 1984), p. 10. All subsequent references are to this edition.

2. Jacques Lacan, *Ecrits: A Selection*, trans. Alan Sheridan (New York, 1977), p. 4.

3. Ibid.

4. Ibid., p. 86.

5. Jacques Lacan, 'Some Reflections on the Ego', *International Journal of Psychoanalysis*, 34 (1953), 15.

6. Jane Gallop, *Reading Lacan* (Ithaca, 1985), p. 121.

7. Lacan, *Ecrits*, p. 6.

8. Francis Fergusson, *The Idea of a Theater* (Princeton, 1949), p. 13.

9. Ibid., p. 17.

10. André Green, *The Tragic Effect*, trans. Alan Sheridan (New York, 1979), p. 6.

11. Ibid., p. 7.

12. Ibid., p. 18.

13. Sigmund Freud, 'On Narcissism: An Introduction', *The Standard Edition of the Complete Psychological Works*, trans. James Strachey (London, 1953–74), vol. 14, p. 74.

11

Gender in Transition: 'Waiting for Godot' and 'Endgame'

MARY BRYDEN

'WAITING FOR GODOT'

The pursuant of gender patterning within Beckett's drama is faced with an uncomfortable yet fascinating question. Indeed, perhaps its very appeal derives from precisely the resistance mounted by the products of a sixty-year writing career to incorporation within a gender-orientated taxonomy. This may be why existing critical writing on the subject tends to gravitate towards analysis of those individual plays, or small clusters of plays – *Not I, Footfalls, Rockaby* – which appear to subject a central female to a noticeably intense scrutiny. Thus, by extension, plays in which women appear on stage either not at all (*Waiting for Godot*), or proportionately little (*Endgame*), have featured only scantily in the gender debate.

Of course, feminist criticism – that umbrella term which tends to shelter all those approaches which take gender as a structuring principle – is itself diverse, and hospitable to an array of methods. Some strands have moved firmly on from the study of women-imaging in male-authored texts: a study which offered initially heady guerrilla activity against a patriarchal and overwhelmingly male canon. Some twenty to thirty years ago, it was enlightening and liberating to excavate and reveal the implicit textual dichotomies which constructed woman as man would have her constituted. More recent deconstructive activity, by Jacques Derrida and others, has further exposed a Western cultural and philosophical heritage in which pervasive oppositions – (male/female; norm/deviation; spirit/ flesh; light/darkness; good/evil; intellect/appetite) – operate such that the privileged first-rank terms ensure the debasement of the second-rank terms. Woman is thus Man-handled into a sequestered schema of dangerous alterity, in which she is associated with all those categories – flesh, appetite, sin, deviation – which share her secondary, 'not-man' status.

Many feminist practitioners have now progressed to the rehabilitative work of resurrecting ignored or forgotten woman-authored literary enterprise, or to the task of identifying and celebrating emergent women's writing. Others choose not to differentiate between gendered producers, and examine the writing of both women and men, using the variety of approaches – psychoanalytical, Marxist, archetypal, mythic, etc. – which have endowed feminist criticism with its undoubted productivity.

One shared assumption amid this eclecticism, however, is the Marxian insight that text cannot operate within a notionally culture-free or ideologically neutral zone. It is for this reason that some feminist critics dismiss *Waiting for Godot* as an all-male play masquerading as universal. Two male wayfarers encounter a further male wayfarer with manservant, and await a macho-sounding Mr Godot who eventually despatches one of two messenger-boys. Cursory advertence to the existence of women occurs in the well-worn alignment of women with the earth and with coition. Thus, Estragon is fond of assuming a foetal posture, and at one point rhapsodises (ironically?): 'Sweet mother earth!'[1] Pozzo too indulges in this feminisation of under-foot matter, savouring the phrase: 'That's how it is on this bitch of an earth' (*WFG*, p. 38) as the climactic coda to his peroration on the dusk and its properties. Further, although Estragon embarks 'voluptuously' (*WFG*, p. 16) upon a story about prostitutes, he is interrupted sharply by Vladimir. The much more (en)durable and attainable fantasy in which they shortly afterwards revel is that of the 'erection' which hanging themselves would produce, with, as Vladimir, adds, 'all that follows' (*WFG*, p. 17). This woman-free ejaculation would, maintains Vladimir, produce mandrakes where it fell.

As with so many jokes from Beckett the linguist, this one has a subtext. The appellation 'man-drake' unites the concepts both of men and menace (Latin *draco* = dragon, serpent), and the mandrake plant, related to the deadly nightshade, has for several thousand years been credited with magical and aphrodisiac qualities. Reputed to shriek when uprooted, its root often resembles a human form. Indeed, popular legend ascribed its propagation to the fallen seed of hanged murderers: hence its peculiar relevance to Didi and Gogo's gallows fantasy. This mythic, onanistic generation proves infinitely less repellent to these wanderers than that which involves coopera- tion with women, for the latter (explicitly female – 'elles' – in the original French) 'give birth astride of a grave' (*WFG*, p. 89). Pozzo's solemn observation is echoed a little later by Vladimir: 'Astride of a grave and a difficult birth' (*WFG*, p. 90). Women's parturient organs are thus seen as weapons of death, for in giving birth they simul- taneously issue an unavoidable expiry date.

On the face of it, then, women (especially fertile ones) are potential agents of disturbance, and are better excluded or (as in many Biblical genealogies) left in the wings, unacknowledged in life-transactions. Indeed, the same Pozzo who refers to birthing women as 'they' is anxious to identify Estragon and Vladimir, infinitely worse for wear than himself at this point, as being 'of the same species' (*WFG*, p. 23). Reciprocally, when in the second act the prone and now blind Pozzo cries for help, Vladimir pontificates that, given only himself and Estragon as proximate first aiders: 'At this moment of time, all mankind is us' (*WFG*, p. 79). Later, when the still writhing Pozzo responds to shouts of both 'Abel' and 'Cain', Estragon is quick to conclude in jocular fashion that affiliation with these two male offspring of Adam and Eve makes of Pozzo 'all humanity' (*WFG*, p. 83).

With women thus excised from the scenario, it would seem that what reigns in their absence is, in Marxian terms, a 'bourgeois' ideology which plasters over opposing factions and promotes a dominant class (adult male) as a universal norm. Further, critics who liken Vladimir and Estragon's plight to a 'universal human predica- ment' are often accused of merely colluding with that prevailing mode of representation in which woman (like worker and child) constitutes the devalued subclass.

It is a persuasive argument, particularly when compounded by familiarity with Beckett's well-known distaste for proposals to stage all-female productions of *Godot*. Yet to harness the play irrefutably to Marx's exposition of the powerful logic of dissimulation seems somehow inadequate. The critique elaborated by Claude Lefort, the French socio-political theorist, is of use here. While giving Marx credit for laying bare the partisan basis of dominant universalising ideologies, Lefort goes on to question what he calls Marx's 'positivism': a presupposition that the division of labour derives from similar division in the sexual act. By means of this assumption, maintains Lefort, Marx is enabled to present as 'naturally' determined 'a division of the sexes in such a way that the partners would naturally identify themselves as different, and hence would naturally come to reflect upon this difference and to represent themselves as man and woman'.[2] If this self-(de)selection be presumed inevitable – and Beckett's play, in a pleasing ambiguity, undoubtedly uses labour (=parturition) as a differentiating factor between the sexes – then *Godot* does appear to confirm a negation of 'female experience' in favour of a totalising male hegemony.

However, as Lefort goes on to argue, social division is not quite so easily compartmentalised into categories to which sexual organs alone provide the basis for admittance. Further, that same distrust of the rhetoric of 'objectivity' leads one to conclude that: 'It would be impossible to take up a position which would enable one to grasp the totality of social relations and the interplay of their articulations' (Lefort, p. 194). For 'social relations' we may here substitute 'gender relations', since gender (unlike sex) is a social category. In the case of Beckett's later (prose and drama) work, where the very notion of a stable selfhood is destabilised, provision must be made for a whole spectrum of sexual, provisionally sexual and sexually indeterminate identities. Moreover, as far as *Waiting for Godot* is concerned, the women to whom Pozzo refers are not woman-as-species, but rather those caught up in that most unenviable process of labour. Within this more heterogeneous conception of gender, it seems that to replace male *Godot* actors with female ones is not necessarily to perform a neatly satisfying exchange of theoretical specificities, as though gender were indisputably indicative of alternative 'essences'.

To explore the question: 'Why (not) women in *Godot*?' is, however, revealing. If to substitute women actors somehow alters the play, it is important to know why. Those who depart from the Marxian assumption that women are, as cultural collectivity, inevitably resident within a differentiated identity will tend to acquiesce with the notion of switched gender betokening alteration, yet will wish to authorise that alteration as politically expedient. (Whether or not assuming men's relinquished shoes is desirable is another matter.) Those, on the other hand, who maintain that such a substitution should make no difference to the play, since women too may alternate as cultural norm, must nevertheless grapple with a certain oddity appertaining to cross-sexual referents such as the 'erection' double-entendre referred to earlier. Moreover, unless the female actors are merely to provide the 'frisson' of possibly trans- vestite women, both camps must accept that textual changes at least – (pronouns, summonses to 'gentlemen', adjectival agreements in the case of French) – are indicated.

No dramatist is likely to welcome the prospect of textual changes being made to his/her artefact on another's initiative. It is therefore convenient for the purposes of argument to subtract henceforth the authorial presence from this discussion. Not before noting, however, one small but significant comment made very recently by Beckett. In a café interview with Ahmad Kamyabi Mask, Beckett responded to a question from his interlocutor as follows:[3]

> 'You refused to let women play *Waiting for Godot* in Germany. Why?'
> 'What does it matter!' He started laughing, reflected and then said, in humorous vein, 'Because women don't have a prostate'. He repeated this three times and burst out laughing, adding: 'Therefore, they can't play a man's role. It's a play written for men'.

On one level, this amusement at the idea of gender inclusiveness might be deemed offensive to women. Beyond that level, however, the self-justification deserves serious attention, despite its levity of expression. It is notable that the men in question are by no means the triumphant guardians of patriarchal dominance. Far from defining female as *lack* in relation to a central phallic signifier, Beckett's remarks implicitly align the males of *Godot* with disorders in precisely that function. Within Beckett's humorous rendering, women are said to lack not the phallus but the prostate gland – malfunction of which constitutes not a gynaecological but what might be called an 'andrological' disorder: a disorder from which Vladimir, for one, quite clearly suffers.[4]

Neither are the males of *Godot* wielders of anything resembling patriarchal power. Beckett's project unfolds itself in a sparse life- space in which power is haphazard, unreliable, and apparently not derived from gender membership. Had the emiserated, whipped, luckless Lucky been conceived as a woman, this argument would be difficult to sustain. As it is, it becomes possible to suggest that the fact that the wayfarers on this particular country road are all male could just conceivably – though perhaps only just – be devoid of statistical significance. Their greater significance appears to lie not in any normative status but in their very contingency and apparent dispensability.

Moreover, as Pozzo's material and physical deterioration demonstrates, these males may be alive and kicking – (the latter an art in which they are skilled) – but only precariously so. They have *space* (inhospitable though it may be), but no *place*. Or rather, their momentary tenure of that place is constantly threatened by poverty, illness, or gang warfare. In one sense one can here couple Beckett, the generator of the written text, with Vladimir, Estragon *et al.*, the generators of the spoken text. Thus *Godot*'s repeated refrain 'Nothing to be done' is paralleled by the writer's espousal, in his *Three Dialogues* with Georges Duthuit, of 'the expression that there is nothing to express, nothing with which to express, nothing from which to express, no power to express, no desire to express, together with the obligation to express' (*Three Dialogues*, p. 103). This shared destitution is interestingly developed by Philip Beitchman when he contends that: 'The modernist writer who "knows nothing" is the functional equivalent of the proletarian who "has nothing"'.[5]

While possibly appearing temporarily to have departed from the gender focus, my argument nevertheless aims to show that the 'wall-to-wall' maleness of *Godot*, far from enshrining any dominant male power-base, in fact participates in a dynamic of contingency and under-privilege in which gender is an unremarkable detail. Interestingly, in an essay taking the form of a tribute to Beckett, the prolific French feminist writer and academic, Hélène Cixous, singles out for mention both the 'extreme poverty' of Beckett's writing and its dismantling of gender predictors.[6] Indeed, the extraordinary Beckett-inspired para-text which concludes her essay caresses at length the notion of gender fluidity, and projects, through the imagined voice of Beckett, the observation that: 'All becoming is a struggle. What interests me is to pass from begun to beginnings. From inseminated to insemination' (Cixous, p. 413). In this fashion Cixous presents sexual identity in Beckett's work as freed from any essentialist straitjacket which might seek to preserve gender hierarchies.

In this context I would want to argue that, if the males of *Godot* are seen as normative, then such an attribution does not derive from their maleness, but from their hapless presence on that stark life-scape which may or may not be included in the cosmic eye-sweep. All-female productions are not thereby invalidated – (though sexual/

textual incongruities are, as we have seen earlier, productive of inconvenience) – but are perhaps rendered unnecessary, even on political grounds of integration. Moreover, despite Pozzo's allocation of the pronoun 'they' to women, the stigma of birth is attached not so much to the female birthers as to the renewed prospect of another organism beginning a life-sentence. As the birthing women squat astride the grave, says Vladimir: 'The air is full of our cries' (WFG, p. 91). The cries, one might propose, are from reluctant female and male participants alike.

To conclude, then, Godot is not a male clique which struts in seclusion from the female. The voices encountered here are too bruised, too hedged about by randomness, to be charged with hogging the space. One suspects that the indifference which Mr Godot reputedly displays to those hanging (or aspiring to hang) on his words is no respecter of either persons or genders.

'ENDGAME'

The majority of the figures in Beckett's stage and media plays are of discernible gender (though the exceptions, such as the scurrying figures of Quad or the djellaba-clad Auditor of Not I, should not be overlooked). However, what distinguishes the stage women from a great many of those inscribed in Beckett's early fiction is that their gender is relieved of any weight of biologistic essentialism. In other words, though often superficially conventional – witness Nell's lacy cap in Endgame, Winnie's lipstick in Happy Days – these women are subject to the same suffering, the same incomprehension, the same recurrent unease with their life-occupancy as the males. Both males and females feel the same restlessness in their bodies which, while degenerate, still play host to a mind painfully aware of its own entrapment. The route is full of setbacks for all, and women struggle with or without men in a hostile environment in which comradeship is sometimes a boon, sometimes a curse.

Nell and Nagg, the bin-bound parents of Hamm in Endgame, do seem to demonstrate a solidarity which transcends the metal barriers between them. Moreover, when Nell falls lengthily silent, Nagg is reported by Clov to be silently crying in his can, still clinging to life, like the male bird in Rough for Theatre II, who perseveres in singing even when his mate is lying dead in the cage.

Indeed, Nell in Endgame is last to speak and first to fall silent.

Nevertheless, hers is not a minor part. She shares with Hamm, Clov and Nagg the painful tension between the need for human contact and the consciousness of the inescapable solitude of the individual. When Nell, in her first words, enquires: 'What is it, my pet? Time for love?' (*E*, p. 18), the only human intercourse available is verbal. Nell and Nagg can no longer touch each other, and can see each other 'hardly' (*E*, p. 18). Moreover, even to converse requires that they unseal their bins and expose themselves to a chill air which renders them respectively 'perished' and 'freezing' (*E*, p. 19).

What, then, might at first be imagined to be a communion of co-sufferers and even co-comforters in this skull-space turns out in fact to be merely four people oppressed by forces largely beyond their control, and unable to provide salvation for either themselves or others. *Endgame* is not a play about giving comfort, on the part of either males or females, and Beckett saw no need to apologise for the fact. With reference to those who proposed elucidatory readings for these frayed remains, Beckett remarked: 'If people want to have headaches among the overtones, let them. And provide their own aspirin'.[7]

Indeed, for all its heavy pessimism, *Endgame* is not a play which encourages uniform readings. Completely absent from the play is what Claude Lefort refers to as the pervasive 'invisible ideology' which envelops people with an insulating cocoon and which provides (often by means of the mass media) 'the constant illusion of a *between-us*, an *entre-nous*' (Lefort, p. 228). Thus, by attunement to a common stimulus, whether it be background music, group therapy, radio or television, each person may gain access to 'a hallucination of *nearness* which abolishes a sense of distance, strangeness, imperceptibility, the signs of the outside, of adversity, of otherness' (Lefort, p. 228). No such mutual analgesia is available to the *Endgame* players – not even the aspirin which Beckett recommends to the critical constituencies, for there's 'no more pain-killer. You'll never get any more pain-killer' (*E*, p. 46). Nell, though gentle, elegiac and seemingly devoid of acrimony, is nevertheless clearsightedly candid about the weariness ensuing from being the continual butt of unhappiness: 'Nothing is funnier than unhappiness, I grant you that ... And we laugh, we laugh, with a will, in the beginning. But it's always the same thing' (*E*, p. 20).

As in *Godot*, recognition of shared adversity, even brave amusement in the face of it, fail to provide a permanent remedy, and both camaraderie and interpersonal conflict can only alternate with that interior angst whose root is deeply personal. It is to deal with this latter turmoil that each character in *Endgame* – and Nell is no exception – clings to remote imaginative spaces or time-spans. While Hamm dreams of running into the woods, Clov of 'a world where all would be silent and still' (*E*, p. 39), and Nagg of the day when Hamm will call out to him in need as he did when a small boy, Nell is lost in contemplation of: 'ah, yesterday!' (*E*, pp. 18, 20). While lodged upon a layer of dirty sand, she nevertheless dreams of clear, bright desert sand. Indeed, her last audible word, before being rammed back by Clov into the darkness of her ashcan is 'Desert!' (*E*, p. 22).

In this, Nell can be compared to another Nell, that of Dickens' *The Old Curiosity Shop*,[8] who, fallen upon misfortune, sits 'still and motionless' in the 'cold and gloomy' chamber (*TOCS*, p. 68), but who, rousing to reverie, recalls happier times with her grandfather and envisions a scene akin to that of her Beckettian namesake: 'Sun, and stream, and meadow, and summer days, shone brightly in her view, and there was no dark tint in all the sparkling picture' (*TOCS*, p. 93). Both Nells embark on long journeys in which they damage their legs: Nell in *Endgame* remembers how she and Nagg travelled one behind the other and met with misfortune 'when we crashed on our tandem and lost our shanks' (*E*, p. 19), whereas little Nell's grandfather relates how, with her bare feet cut and bruised by stones, she 'walked behind me . . . that I might not see how lame she was' (*TOCS*, p. 520).

As we have seen, the last we hear of *Endgame*'s Nell is when she is pushed firmly down into her bin. Its lid is then replaced, and Hamm enquires of Clov: 'Have you bottled her?' Receiving an affirmative reply, he recommends: 'Screw down the lids' (*E*, p. 22). Dickens' Nell comes to a similar end. Taken to the dark church crypt by the sexton, she terms it: 'A black and dreadful place!' (*TOCS*, p. 402), and is invited to peer into a vault, its lid uplifted. Later, after her death, her body is removed to that same vault, which is then 'covered and the stone fixed down' (*TOCS*, p. 529). Doubt attaches in both cases to the moment of death. It is never established definitively that *Endgame*'s Nell is dead: merely that it 'looks like it' (*E*, p. 41). Similarly, it is stated of little Nell that: 'They did not know that she was dead, at first' (*TOCS*, p. 525). However, the presences of both appear to linger after the cessation of their voice. The villagers linger in the snow in *The Old Curiosity Shop*, 'coming to the grave in little knots, and glancing down' (*TOCS*, p. 529), and, long after Nell's silencing, Nagg requests two sugar-plums: 'One for me and one for – ' (*E*, p. 35), the blank denoting his absent wife, whose pulse trace has become a straight line. Then, after hearing from Hamm that there are no more sugar-plums, Nagg perseveres in attending upon Nell's bin-lid, knocking on it and calling her name in hope of a response which, if given, is never heard.

The temporary linkage above of Nell and little Nell is suggested here in tentative fashion as productive of a few interesting parallels. Beckett is known, moreover, to have read Dickens widely, and not only makes (both veiled and explicit) reference to his work in the early unpublished *Dream of Fair to Middling Women*, but also speaks approvingly in the essay *Dante . . . Bruno, Vico . . . Joyce* of his robustly vivid descriptive powers: 'We hear the ooze squelching all through Dickens's description of the Thames in *Great Expectations*'.[9] In this context, it would be inconceivable that Beckett would be unfamiliar with the character of little Nell. However, as with all such inter-textual resonances in the case of Beckett, it must eventually be laid aside, for, whereas Dickens leaves the reader with the comforting assurance that: 'Of every tear that sorrowing mortals shed on such green graves, some good is born' (*TOCS*, p. 529), the only solace which results from Nagg's tears is a biscuit to suck in seclusion. Moreover, this crypt contains no 'green graves', for, as Hamm surmises: 'We're down in a hole. But beyond the hills? Eh? Perhaps it's still green' (*E*, p. 30).

Nevertheless, in a sense, Nell's impulse to brightness retains its powerful association, for Hamm, after hearing of Nell's probable death, commands: 'Bring me under the window. I want to feel the light on my face' (*E*, p. 42). After all, as Clov later reminds him in connection with the mysterious Mother Pegg who 'was bonny once, like a flower of the field' (*E*, p. 31), the inability to procure lamp oil – the means to induce light – can invite more than darkness: 'You know what she died of, Mother Pegg? Of darkness' (*E*, p. 48). It seems probable that the retracted Nagg too will soon succumb to the darkness, for, as Hamm callously observes: 'The dead go fast' (*E*, p. 44). In this process, once again, gender membership is of no relevance or influence.

In the final analysis the difficulty in finding an equilibrium between human partnership needs and individual imperatives is never re-solved in this play. While, as we have seen, each participant has a memory-refuge and/or a rich fantasy life, the merit of this facility – that it insulates self from other in a flight of enjoyable escapism – is counterbalanced by its penalty of sealing the dreamer off from his/ her co-locutors. Thus, Nell, deep in her recollections of the 'so white' lake (*E*, p. 21), is oblivious to Nagg's laboriously-told story about the tailor, at the conclusion of which he alone 'breaks into a high forced laugh' (*E*, p. 22). Similarly, Clov misunderstands Nell's lyrical outburst: 'Desert!' and, assuming its meaning to be: 'She told me to go away, into the desert' (*E*, p. 22), roughly reseals her into the bin from which she never again emerges.

So no concessions or privileges are observable on grounds of gender in this play. Indeed, though observable, gender membership appears to be not only random but also immaterial, and other instances in *Endgame* compound this impression. When Clov gives various details to the blind Hamm about the toy dog the latter wishes to have positioned in front of him, the dog's sexual organs are seemingly regarded as a bothersome detail, on a par with the neck-ribbon, to be added as a finishing touch:

> **Hamm** You've forgotten the sex.
> **Clov** But he isn't finished. The sex goes on at the end.
> (*E*, p. 30)

The important function of the dog is, as Hamm instructs, to be left propped on its three legs 'gazing at me' and 'imploring me' (*E*, p. 31). Its denoted sexual capacity is thus subsidiary to its inter-relational potential. As such, it merely adds gender indeterminacy to the imagined sexual sterility it shares with Nagg and Nell, no longer able to reach each other to kiss, and with Clov and Hamm. For the latter, memories of sexual activity are now past, the stuff of nothing more than a 'reminiscent leer' in tribute to Mother Pegg, who was 'bonny once . . . And a great one for the men!' (*E*, p. 31). For Clov, moreover, a human touch is now unthinkable, and he repulses decisively Hamm's appeal for an embrace: 'I won't kiss you anywhere . . . I won't touch you' (*E*, p. 44). In a barren, post-sexual world, all he can discern is 'between my legs a little trail of black dust' (*E*, p. 51).

In such an environment, where physical and psychic insecurity are high, the need to specify and record gender patterns has already receded. At one point, Hamm describes a desperate man who, on Christmas Eve, 'came crawling towards me, on his belly. Pale, wonderfully pale and thin'. The man raises his face, which is 'black with mingled dirt and tears' and begs for 'bread for his brat' (*E*, pp. 35–6). In so doing, he identifies the child's gender in a manner which infuriates Hamm, who recalls venomously: 'My little boy, he said, as if the sex mattered' (*E*, p. 36).

An echo of this comment occurs in the original French *Fin de partie*, when, towards the close of the play, Clov reports picking out through his telescope a small, immobile figure outside. In the English version, the figure is said to resemble 'a small boy' (*E*, p. 49), his movement pattern is not mentioned, and the topic is speedily abandoned. The exchange is, however, considerably expanded in the French original (*FP*, pp. 103–5), where, apropos of this 'quelqu'un' [somebody], Hamm enquires: 'Sexe?' and receives the reply: 'Quelle importance?' [What does it matter?]. (Clov's reply, interestingly, is identical to that given by Beckett to the question posed by Ahmad Kamyabi Mask, cited earlier, concerning the suggested female/male substitution in *Godot* productions.) After this displayed indifference to gender configurations, Clov goes on in the French version to refer to the object of curiosity as 'un môme' [a kid, brat], and the question of gender is suspended (though Clov thereafter styles the apparition 'il' – the masculine pronoun – presumably for convenience). The figure, upon further examination, appears to be sitting on the ground, leaning against an object. That object, intervenes Hamm, is 'la pierre levée' [the raised stone]. By using the definite article 'la', Hamm makes allusion to the rolled-away stone described in Gospel accounts as a sign of the resurrection of Christ. No such life-renewal will occur in *Endgame*'s landscape, however, for Hamm declares that the figure is perhaps dead, and/or will die eventually in any case. Thus, this outer being, unable to procreate, is of no further threat or even interest. Its gender is as immaterial as its doubtful existence, which is itself made subject to that dead-line which Hamm chooses to describe in the reported death-words of Christ: 'C'est fini' [It is finished].

To sum up, both *Waiting for Godot* and *Endgame* represent a significant moment in the development of gender inscription in Beckett's writing. Behind them, among the wordier surroundings of Beckett's early prose work, lie a multitude of women who are grounded in alterity, in what is viewed by the central male narrator as awkward divergence. Short stories such as *First Love* or those included in the early collection *More Pricks Than Kicks* are prime examples of this. Moreover, the later 'woman-plays' to which we have referred lie many years ahead. It is at this early point in Beckett's writing for the theatre – that stage marked by *Waiting for*

Godot and *Endgame* – that the objectified female referent begins to fade. Indeed, gender begins to shed any consistency as a predictor of behaviour or attitude. Such static essentialism becomes in fact the first casualty of a radically transformed self-epiphany.

It would be difficult to sustain such an argument on the evidence of *Waiting for Godot* alone. Indeed, as we have seen, the play is often justifiably under pressure from without when projected as male preserve rather than as luckless misadventure. Nonetheless, it is *Godot* which presents one of the most startling images of that deterritorialisation which unsettles all stabilities of expectation. Included in those destabilisations is that of gender. Moreover, as *Endgame* proceeds to demonstrate, that dissolution of genderised apartheid is not so much a function of pressure towards integration as of an intense recognition of the mutuality (and yet, in the end, the solitude) attendant upon the life-predicament. That predicament is thus to be avoided, for birth reactivates the weary cycle of pain. Yet women are no longer reviled as the prime culprits in the sin of reproduction, as so often in Beckett's early writing. Pozzo in *Waiting for Godot* undoubtedly makes it clear, as we have noted, that birth is a regrettable occurrence in which women are the delivery agents. Nevertheless, they – 'Elles' – do not receive the opprobrium directed at them in Beckett's earlier work. Indeed, in *Endgame*, both parents are regarded by their offspring, Hamm, with equal indifference: 'My father? My mother? My ... dog?' (*E*, p. 12). Furthermore, it is his father whom he singles out at one point as his 'accursed progenitor' (*E*, p. 15).

What is remarkable about both these plays, therefore, is not any supposed rehabilitation of women, but rather their steady erasure of specificity from gender patterning, such that male and female alike, divorced from any notion of privilege, can be seen to struggle as best they may in a tattered world. In such circumstances, Hamm's bitter gibe: 'As if the sex mattered' (*E*, p. 36) begins to seem more apposite than perverse. Of course, in thus experimenting with sexual indifference, Beckett runs the risk of attracting accusations of tolerating that phenomenon of female 'invisibility' with which many women are only too familiar. Yet the visible/invisible dichotomy can only remain functional and convincing if the 'other' sex – male – is contrastingly prominent and pre-eminent. As we have seen, if any seen/unseen dialectic exists, it does not render consistent or fruitful data in association with gender distribution by this stage in Beckett's writing. Moreover, the slackening hold on gender determinism which these plays display points forward to a succession of later drama and prose in which gender as a categoriser retreats, along with other organising categories, to cede to the all-encompassing quest of the fragmenting yet persisting self.

NOTES

[Mary Bryden's essay has been specially written for this volume. It is an excellent example of one of the most interesting and important new developments in Beckett criticism, namely the exploration by feminist critics of the representation of gender (as well as, one might say, the gendering of representation) in Beckett's work. This marks a departure from traditional criticism which has tended to be blind or indifferent to Beckett's gender-distinctions or to take the experience of male protagonists in that work as universal. Much valuable work has already been done on the representation of women and women's language in Beckett's work. Here, rather than taking that more predictable route, Bryden looks closely at the meaning and value of maleness in *Waiting for Godot* and *Endgame*. Ed.]

1. *Waiting for Godot* (London, 1965). All references will be to this edition, abbreviated to *WFG*, and inserted parenthetically in the text. References to other texts by Beckett are as follows: *E: Endgame* (London, 1958); *FP: Fin de partie* (Paris, 1957); *M: Murphy* (London, 1973); *Three Dialogues: Proust and Three Dialogues With Georges Duthuit* (London, 1965); *W: Watt* (New York, 1956).

2. Claude Lefort, 'Outline of the Genesis of Ideology in Modern Societies' (originally published as 'Esquisse d'une genèse de l'ideologie dans les sociétés modernes', *Textures*, 8–9 [1974]), trans. John B. Thompson, in *The Political Forms of Modern Society: Bureaucracy, Democracy, Totalitarianism*, ed. John B. Thompson (Cambridge, 1986), pp. 181–236. See p. 193. References hereafter will be to 'Lefort' and inserted parenthetically in the text.

3. Ahmad Kamyabi Mask, *Dernière Rencontre avec Samuel Beckett* (Paris, 1990), p. 23 (my translation).

4. Nevertheless, female actors playing *Godot* might well counter Beckett's identification of prostate disorder with maleness by reference to his own footnote attaching to the doleful medical history of the Lynch family in *Watt*: 'Haemophilia is, like enlargement of the prostate, an exclusively male disorder. *But not in this work*' (*W*, p. 102, my italics: I am indebted to Steven Connor for reminding me of this passage). This, the argument might go, could be seen as authorial use of the 'female' characteristics defined by Murphy: 'Women are really extraordinary, the way they want to give their cake to the cat and have it' (*M*, p. 114).

5. Philip Beitchman, *I Am A Process With No Subject* (Gainesville, 1988), p. 278.

6. Hélène Cixous, 'Une passion: l'un peu moins que rien', in *Cahier de l'Herne: Samuel Beckett*, ed. T. Bishop and R. Federman (Paris, 1976), pp. 396–413. References hereafter will be to 'Cixous' and inserted parenthetically in the text.

7. Extract from letter to Alan Schneider, 29 December 1957, quoted in *Disjecta: Miscellaneous Writings and a Dramatic Fragment*, ed. Ruby Cohn (London, 1983), p. 109.

8. Everyman edition of *The Old Curiosity Shop* (London, 1907). References hereafter will be to *TOCS* and inserted parenthetically in the text.

9. This essay (which first appeared in *Our Exagmination Round His Factification for Incamination of Work in Progress* [Paris, 1929] and in *transition*, 16–17) appears in *Disjecta*, pp. 19–33. See p. 28.

Further Reading

In what follows, I have tried to indicate the most interesting and useful ways to follow up the essays gathered together here with criticism directed towards *Waiting for Godot* or *Endgame*. However, many of the most interesting new approaches to Beckett's work have been exemplified in work that treats these two plays alongside Beckett's other writing, or, indeed, in work that concentrates on other plays. I have included examples of such work in this further reading section in the interests of illustrating as wide a range of approaches as possible and in hope of encouraging students to read more widely in Beckett's writing both for the stage and for the page.

BECKETT AND LANGUAGE

Much contemporary literary theory is characterised by the centrality in it of the question of language. This is especially, but not exclusively true of post-structuralist or deconstructive accounts.

Jean Alter, 'Waiting for the Referent: Waiting for Godot? (On Referring in Theatre)', in *On Referring in Literature*, ed. Anna Whiteside and Michael Assacharoff (Bloomington: Indiana University Press, 1987), pp. 42–56. A rigorous semiotic, or structuralist account of *Waiting for Godot*.

Roger Bishop, 'Beckett and the Language of the Void', *Southwest Journal of Linguistics*, 7:1 (1984), 16–25.

Rethinking Beckett: A Collection of Critical Essays, ed. Lance St. John Butler and Robin J. Davis (Basingstoke: Macmillan, 1990), gathers together a range of essays informed in different ways by poststructuralist theory. It is mostly focused on Beckett's later work.

Steven Connor's *Samuel Beckett: Repetition, Theory and Text* (Oxford: Blackwell, 1988) draws on the work of Jacques Derrida and Gilles Deleuze to offer a deconstructive account of the whole range of Beckett's work.

Waiting for Godot and *Endgame* have recently attracted a number of studies informed by the insights of the 'speech-act theory' originating in the work of J. L. Austin and extended by John Searle. This theory suggests that language is best thought of as a form of social action, rather than simply as the imparting or communication of meaning. The following are examples of essays which examine Beckett's dramatic language in terms of speech-act theory:

Manuela Corfanù and Daniela Roventa-Frumusani, 'Absurd Dialogue and Speech Acts in Beckett's *En Attendant Godot*', *Poetics*, 13 (1984), 119–33.

Kripa K. Gautam and Manjula Sharma, 'Dialogue in *Waiting for Godot* and Grice's Concept of Implicature', *Modern Drama*, 29:4 (1986), 580–6.

R. A. York, 'Presuppositions and Speech Acts in Beckett's *Fin de Partie*', *Proceedings of the Royal Irish Academy*, 83 (1983), 239–50.

BECKETT AND POSTMODERNISM

Beckett's work has been central to the synoptic and fluidly transformative accounts of postmodernism offered by Ihab Hassan. Students should see especially his *The Literature of Silence: Henry Miller and Samuel Beckett* (New York: Alfred A. Knopf, 1967) and the essay 'Joyce-Beckett: A Scenario in 8 scenes and a Voice', in *Paracriticisms: Seven Speculations of the Times* (Urbana: University of Illinois Press, 1975), pp. 63–73.

Students might also be interested to consult Maria M. Brewer, 'Samuel Beckett: Postmodern Narrative and the Nuclear *Telos*', in *boundary 2*, 14:i–ii (1986–7), pp. 153–70.

BECKETT AND POLITICS

Thomas J. Cousineau, '*Waiting for Godot* and Politics', in *Coriolan: Théatre et Politique*, ed. Jean P. Debax and Yves Peyré (Toulouse, 1984), pp. 161–7.

Peter Gidal, *Understanding Beckett: A Study of Monologue and Gesture in the Works of Samuel Beckett* (Basingstoke: Macmillan, 1986). This is a demanding, sometimes rather obscure book, but it is nevertheless a highly suggestive account of the political significance of Beckett's material practice in the theatre.

MANUSCRIPT AND THEATRICAL RESEARCH

A great deal of evidence exists of Beckett's methods of composition and manner of directing his own plays, and this has begun to exercise an influence on criticism of his work.

Stanley E. Gontarski, *The Intent of Undoing in Samuel Beckett's Texts* (Bloomington: University of Indiana Press, 1985) is a hugely illuminating study of the early stages of composition of Beckett's plays, including a chapter on *Endgame*.

There has been a great deal of interesting recent work dealing with Beckett's practice as a director of his own plays. If it is true that little of this is informed directly by new theoretical approaches, the question of the relationship between text and performance is one that may be interestingly illuminated by the deconstructive, reader-centred and gender-based accounts exemplified in this volume. Martha Fehsenfeld and Dugald Macmillan, *Beckett in the Theatre: The Author as Practical Playwright and Director: Vol. 1: Waiting for Godot to Krapp's Last Tape* (London: John Calder, 1988), is full of fascinating information about Beckett's methods of directing *Waiting for Godot* and *Endgame*, among other plays. Another consideration of Beckett as director of his own work is to be found in Colin Duckworth, 'Beckett's New *Godot*', in *Beckett's Later Fiction and Drama: Texts For Company*, ed. James Acheson and Kateryna Archer (New York: St. Martin's 1987), pp. 175–92.

OTHER APPROACHES

Shimon Levy, *Samuel Beckett's Self-Referential Drama: The Three 'I's* (Basingstoke: Macmillan, 1990). This draws on the work of Paul Ricoeur and Wolfgang Iser to develop a 'hermeneutic' approach to Beckett's drama. This approach emphasises that Beckett's dramatic self-reflexiveness, his insistence on making us recognise that we are watching a play rather than a depiction of the real, induces a parallel self-consciousness in the reader/spectator.

Sidney Homan, *Beckett's Theaters: Interpretations for Performance* (Lewisburg: Bucknell University Press; London and Toronto: Associated University Presses, 1984), argues that Beckett's plays depend on the enactment of meaning and significance in the immediacy of the dramatic situation.

The essays in *Myth and Ritual in the Plays of Samuel Beckett*, ed. Katherine H. Burkman (Rutherford: Fairleigh Dickinson University Press, 1987) draw on a number of contemporary theories of myth, ritual and game to interpret Beckett's plays. *Waiting for Godot* and *Endgame* are treated in particular in the following essays: Lois More Overbeck, 'Ritual as Façon in Beckett's Plays', pp. 21–7; Susan D. Brienza, 'Perilous Journeys on Beckett's Stages: Traveling Through Words', 28–49; Susan Maughlin, 'Liminality: An Approach to Artistic Process in *Endgame*', pp. 86–99; and Claudia Clausius, 'Bad Habits While Waiting for Godot: The Demythification of Ritual', pp. 124–43.

Notes on Contributors

Mary Bryden is Samuel Beckett Research Fellow at the University of Reading, where she divides her time between research work in the Beckett Archive and teaching in the French Studies Department. Her PhD thesis was entitled ' "Another Like Herself"? Women in the Prose and Drama of Samuel Beckett', and she has published articles on gender in Beckett's work. Her related interests are in the field of French theories of the feminine and, in particular, in the work of Hélène Cixous.

James L. Calderwood is Professor of English and Comparative Literature and Associate Dean of Humanities at the University of California, Irvine. He has published a number of books on Shakespeare, most recently *Shakespeare and the Denial of Death* (Amherst, 1988) and *The Properties of Othello* (Amherst, 1989).

Steven Connor is Reader in Modern English Literature and Director of the Centre for Interdisciplinary Research in Culture and the Humanities at Birkbeck College, University of London. He is the author of *Charles Dickens* (Oxford, 1985), *Samuel Beckett, Repetition, Theory and Text* (Oxford, 1988), *Postmodernist Culture: An Introduction to Theories of the Contemporary* (Oxford, 1989) and *Theory and Cultural Value* (Oxford, 1992).

Jane Alison Hale is Assistant Professor of French and Comparative Literature at Brandeis University. She is the author of *The Broken Window: Beckett's Dramatic Perspective* (West Lafayette, Ind., 1987) and *The Lyric Encyclopaedia of Raymond Queneau* (Ann Arbor, 1989). She is currently preparing a study of the Gilles de Rais figure in contemporary French fiction.

Sylvie Debevec Henning is Associate Professor of French and Chair of the Department of Foreign Languages and Literature at the State University of New York in Plattsburgh. Her book, *Beckett's Critical Complicity: Carnival, Contestation and Tradition* (Lexington, 1988) won the 1987 Midwest Modern Language Association Book Award. She has also published a monography, *Genet's Ritual Play*, as well as many reviews and articles on

168

twentieth-century French literature. She is currently working on a study of Beckett's novelistic responses to scepticism.

Wolfgang Iser is Professor of English Literature at the University of Konstanz. He is the author of many critical and theoretical studies, including *The Act of Reading: A Theory of Aesthetic Response* (London, 1978), *The Implied Reader: Patterns of Communication in Prose Fiction from Bunyan to Beckett* (Baltimore, 1974), *Laurence Sterne* (Cambridge, 1988) and *Prospecting: From Reader Response to Literary Anthropology* (Baltimore, 1989).

Andrew K. Kennedy is Professor of English Literature at the University of Bergen and a Life Member of Clare Hall, Cambridge. His publications include *Six Dramatists in Search of a Language* (Cambridge, 1975) and *Dramatic Dialogue* (Cambridge, 1983) as well as short fiction.

Paul Lawley is Senior Lecturer in English at Polytechnic South West (Exmouth). He has published articles on Beckett's drama and prose in several journals and books. He is also the author of numerous articles on other contemporary plays and playwrights.

Jeffrey Nealon is Assistant Professor of English at Pennsylvania State University. He obtained his PhD from Loyola University, Chicago, for a dissertation entitled 'The "Logic" of Postmodernism', concerning the North American reception of postmodern theory. He has essays on aspects of this question forthcoming in *Cultural Critique*, *boundary 2* and *PMLA*, as well as a book, *Double Reading*, forthcoming from Cornell University Press.

Judith Roof teaches film, drama and feminist critical studies at the University of Delaware. She is co-editor of *Feminism and Psychoanalysis* (Ithaca and London, 1989) and author of *A Lure of Knowledge: Lesbian Sexuality and Theory* (New York, 1991). In addition to work on Beckett, she has also published essays on Harold Pinter, Marguerite Duras, Tom Stoppard and Sam Shepard.

Gabriele Schwab is Professor of English and Comparative Literature at the University of California, Irvine. She has published two books in German, *Samuel Becketts Endspiel mit der Subjektivität* (Stuttgart, 1981) and *Entgrenzungen und Entgrenzungsmythen*. Her own translation of the latter is forthcoming from Harvard University Press under the title *Subjects Without Selves*. She has published numerous articles on literary theory, modern fiction, women's studies and contemporary culture and is at present completing a book entitled *The Mirror and the Killer-Queen: Reading as an Experience of Otherness*.

Index